WHY GIRLS

CHASE GUYS

AFTER A BREAKUP

Dr. John T. Cocoris

Why Girls Chase Guys After A Breakup

Temperament Dynamics, LLC
2541 S IH 35
STE 200-116
Round Rock, TX 78664

www.temperamentdynamics.com
info@temperamentdynamics.com
512-553-8104

ISBN 978-0-9721650-8-2

Temperament Dynamics, LLC
McKinney, Texas 75072

Cover design by Ty Waldsworth.
Interior design by John T. Cocoris.

For more information go to *www.whygirlschaseguys.com.*

ACKNOWLEDGEMENTS

A special thinks to the three courageous young ladies that were willing to tell their stories. It was not easy for either one to relive their painful experience.

I would like to thank my wife Darrellene, and friend Jodi Williamson, for reading the manuscript offering helpful insights that has made this work better.

Table of Contents

Part ONE

Part TWO

The Stories of Three Girls in Their Own Words

Part THREE

Why Do Girls Chase Guys After A Breakup?

Table of Contents

Part FOUR

How To Move On
With Your Life

PART ONE

INTRODUCTION

Why Was This Book Written?

As a therapist, I have worked with teenage girls and young ladies in their twenties and beyond who demonstrated extreme behavior (including self-harm) and chased guys after a breakup that was not of their choosing. This book was written to answer the question that I've been asked by many of these young ladies, "Why did I do that?"

This work identifies the core issues that drive these young ladies and adults to not let go of a toxic relationship.

If you are holding this book in your hands, you may be a girl looking for answers that would explain your emotions and behavior after a breakup. You may be a parent who is looking to understand your daughter's behavior after a failed relationship. You may also, of course, just be interested in the subject.

The extremes to which some teenagers and adults go to restore a broken relationship are found in the stories of three girls in their own words. The reasons why a girl would demonstrate such extreme behavior are explored. I will offer some guidance that will help you move on with your life if you have had, or you are currently having, this experience.

Much has been written about the reasons why some girls will not give up on a toxic relationship. I will address some of the reasons most write about but I will also introduce my own observations from a viewpoint that no one has written about, specifically, a particular temperament that these girls share.

As I will discuss, *temperament* represents a system that is thousands of years old but offers more insight into behavior than anything else I have found. As a therapists for over three decades, I have never seen a young lady (or guy) with another *temperament* do the extremes things covered in this book. Girls (and guys) with another *temperament* will struggle, but not to this extent and not for an extended period of time.

Another reason to write this book is to let the girls (and their loved ones) know that their emotional display is common and that others have had a similar experience, so you are not alone!

All three girls whose stories are in this book came to me because of such a breakup. They have all agreed to tell their stories published in this work.

I am deeply grateful to these three young ladies that were willing to share their thoughts and feelings during and after a traumatic breakup. To be willing, open, and transparent about their experience was, to say the least, courageous. They had to relive the painful events to write their story. Without their willingness to share their story this book would not have the impact you will experience. The girls are motivated by the desire to help prevent others from the pain that they have experienced.

The girls will tell their story in their own words about their behavior. Their stories reflect honesty about their sexual activity and interest. This part of their experience if not included in their stories would not be authentic. This is the way it is.

Because these girls survived an abusive relationship they are deserving of recognition and honor by telling their story. Some things have been changed to protect their identity.

John T. Cocoris
McKinney, Texas

WARNING!

This book tells the stories of three girls and their struggles with their identity, sexual activity, and relationships. They tell it like it is. Their stories are honest, transparent, and revealing. These girls have willingly opened up their hearts to show you the feelings and hurt that they have experienced. To altar or even soften their stories would hide what these girls and countless others go through. If you think that it might be upsetting to read such honesty then you should read no further.

Chapter 1

IS THIS YOUR STORY?

You meet a guy and you are attracted to him. You're able to communicate with him and you start doing "dating things." You enjoy each other's company and you become committed to seeing each other more often.

At some point you both agree that the relationship is *exclusive* and you both decide not to "date" other people. All is well, or so it appears, and you continue to see him for weeks or even months.

Intimate activity with your boyfriend deepens your belief that the relationship is important to him and that it will last. Sometimes, but not always, you will share mutual friends which further deepens your belief that the relationship is on solid ground. You may move in with him.

Then the abuse starts or becomes more obvious to you. It may have been there before but you dismissed it thinking that he didn't really mean what he said or did. The abuse is most always verbal, sometimes physical, sometimes sexual, but it's clear, he does not respect you ... something is not right!

The abuse becomes more and more a routine part of your relationship with him. He begins to blame you for everything and does not accept accountability for his behavior. You begin to run out of excuses and find it harder and harder to explain his actions to your friends and family.

Your friends (and family members) tell you he's not a good guy but you don't listen. You begin to pull away from those close to you. You then find out he has cheated on you! You try to excuse that behavior because "Maybe it was my fault!" You moved out but you came back. Then one day he decides he no longer wants to be exclusive with you because, he says, "We have drifted apart and it's no longer working!" He declares that you need help or medication and you believe him!

Is This Your Reaction?

Upon hearing the news that it is over you can't just let him go. First, you lose control mentally and emotionally! Behavior becomes irrational, radical, even bizarre. You're consumed with how to get him back.

You spend sleepless nights crying. You can't eat or sleep. You can't concentrate or work and you lose your job! Drugs or alcohol help to bury your pain. You become promiscuous, blow up his phone with calls and texts, stalk him, destroy his property, spread lies about him (or the truth), and then beg him to come back!

Out of frustration, or desperation, or to just get his attention, you consider or even try self -harm. You are overwhelmed with what you need to do to get him to change his mind! You decide "I will change, I'll be better to him, I'll respect him more, and I will stop pointing out his faults and I'll get on that medication!"

Some of your behavior gets so out-of-control that you were committed to a mental hospital for evaluation. You were discharged with medication and a diagnosis of being bipolar, depressed, or having an anxiety disorder.

If any part of this sounds like or is similar to your own story, then keep reading.

Chapter 2

REACTION STAGES?

When a guy initiates the break up a series of stages typically follow for the girl. To say the obvious, you may be at a loss for words to explain what just happened!

All of the stages do not always happen nor do they happen in the same order, but many if not most all of the stages are experienced.

Some of the stages last a short period of time while others last for months, or years, and some even a lifetime. The first few stages listed will initially happen in the order shown. The remaining stages will happen, or not, in no particular order. Look for stages that you have experienced or one you may be going through now. Stages are often revisited once you go through the emotion so expect reoccurrence.

1. Denial

Anytime you receive sudden, distressing news of any kind, your first response is almost always shock and disbelief. It's almost impossible to comprehend the reality of what you just heard! To deal with it you immediately *deny* the *reality* of the event. Confusion sets in, "Wait, what did you just say?" Or you follow with, "You're kidding, right?"

Denial is a way of anesthetizing yourself so that you will not be overwhelmed with pain. Denial is also a way of coping by not accepting the fact of what just happened. Actually, when in denial, no one is able to fully comprehend the magnitude of the event that just occurred.

2. Anger Turned *Outward*

The first direction of your anger is usually turned toward the guy who just broke up with you. The emotional display can be expressed in different ways like yelling, screaming, or throwing things at him.

Sometimes the anger is shown in breaking things, usually his things. The longer this stage goes on the more likely you will purge yourself of anything that may remind you of him like pictures, clothes, etc. Here are a few other ways your anger can be expressed:

Revenge. Your emotions turn from shock and denial to thoughts of revenge! Your thoughts are flooded with how you could hurt him the most. Maybe you could date his best friend, or try to get him fired from his job, or run up his credit cards!

Revenge is driven by hate and it is never a good idea. The opposite of love is not hate, it's *indifference*! So, love and hate are both thinking about the same person. Actually, you become like your emotional focus. If you love someone you tend to become like that person in some ways. So, hating him means you will become just like him is some ways! Ugh!

Spread rumors. You lie about him to your mutual friends (or tell them the truth that you've withheld), smear him on social media, or call his family or employer to let them know how he treated you. Your goal is to hurt his reputation.

Block him. You blocked him on your phone and all social media and then ask your friends and family to do the same.

Silence. This shows your utter disgust for his actions. His behavior is so outlandish that it does not deserve words or an emotional response from you. This response is the most difficult for which he must deal. Silence is not a sign of *weakness*, it's a show of *strength*.

3. Anger Turned *Inward*

Some define depression as *anger turned inward.* Here you blame yourself for the loss of the relationship. Actually, you are angry at yourself for causing the breakup to happen (you think).

Withdraw. When depression hits you feel the deep pain of rejection and it paralyzes you. You withdraw from any social activity or communication with others and stay in bed. You do not know what to do or what to say to your friends and family. Instead, you *do* nothing and *say* nothing. You sleep more. You feel trapped.

It's best to not linger long in this stage. Do your best to get up and get out. Take a brief walk, go to a movie, do a kind deed, listen to music. Give yourself some time but do something besides lay in bed.

3. Victim

The anger turned inward needs a place to settle and it's usually in becoming the victim. Here you think, "This is all my fault," or "He did this to me because I deserved it!" or "Why am I always being rejected?" or "Why is life so cruel?" or "Why do bad things always happen to me?"

In the victim stage you overlook the choices you made to be in and/ or stay in the toxic relationship. It didn't happen *to you*, you *allowed* it to happen.

There is power in understanding that you are not a victim. You *chose* to be in the relationship and you can *choose* to get out of the relationship.

4. Escape

Withdrawal alone can be traumatizing. Being isolated is torture because you're left alone with just your thoughts and feelings. Drugs or alcohol may be used to escape the pain or at least help you not to think about what he did. This is never a good idea.

In you feelings of abandonment and rejection your thoughts turn to the possibility of self-harm. To escape, some become promiscuous and have multiple, and brief, sexual encounters.

5. Restoration Plea

Here you make excuses for his behavior! You rationalize away his deplorable treatment of you. You decide it's just not important.

You reason that if you change he will come back. You spend hours pondering how you will change and what you will say to him. You may even run the ideas by a trusted friend or family member. You write out you thoughts preparing to talk to him. You assume all responsibility for *driving him away* and will plead with him to give you a second chance to prove that you will change!

Caution. The plea for restoration can have a hidden motivation. You devise a scheme to get him back so you can break up with him! You just want to have the last say!

6. Jealousy

When the guy finds someone else another tsunami of emotion may hit you. This time it is wrapped around "I wasn't enough! What does she have that I don't? Did she pull him away from me?" This may ignite another round of destructive behavior toward yourself or him or the new girlfriend. It's best to not react this way.

7. Hurt

Being overwhelmed eventually gives way to grieving the loss. You're rid of all that reminded you of him. You've blocked his phone number and removed him from all your social media contacts. You are coming to grips that it is over, it just hurts, you're sad, and your heart is broken.

8. Reality

In this stage, you list all the things that he did expressing just how bad of a person he is. You asks, "Why didn't I admit what I have seen for a long time?" You finally accept reality that he is not a good person.

9. Move On

Based on the reality you have just accepted will enable you to move on with you life. You decide it's time. You may hold on to the memories of how good it could have been but you accept that it will not happen. You find another and better relationship.

Remember, stages are often revisited once you go through the emotion. Do not be surprised if there are reoccurrences.

Chapter 3

THE WARNING SIGNS

Once the girls began to think more clearly they realized that there were signs that the relationship was toxic. The following warning signs came from the many girls that I have worked with over the years.

1. ☐ He made an issue of being respected by me and others.

2. ☐ Prideful! Used the words *respect* and *proud of* a lot.

3. ☐ Arguments happened when he felt slighted or disrespected.

4. ☐ He treated me with disrespect.

5. ☐ My friends and family did not like him.

6. ☐ He was rude to me in public and privately.

7. ☐ He didn't want me to tell others his business.

8. ☐ He became upset if I told anyone anything about him.

9. ☐ He used drugs and alcohol.

10. ☐ His former girlfriends talked bad about him. I thought I was different to him.

11. ☐ I thought I could help him so I ignored his behavior because I felt sorry for him.

12. ☐ He stood me up lots of times. He said he was coming but would not show up.

13. ☐ I was scared of him.

14. ☐ I defended him with my family and friends because I wanted to prove that I was right about him.

15. ☐ He had very selfish friends.

16. ☐ His friends were more important than me. He was their ring leader.

17. ☐ He expected me to always be there when he wanted me.

18. ☐ Spent selective time with me. Something would always pull him away.

19. ☐ He never took accountability for his behavior. Nothing was ever his fault!

20. ☐ He was too sensitive. He would get mad over the smallest things.

21. ☐ He was violent at times.

22. ☐ He used me for his sexual pleasure. He was not always interested in satisfying me.

23. ☐ He isolated me from my family and friends.

24. ☐ He turned me against *my* family.

25. ☐ He isolated me from *his* family.

26. ☐ He was a mama's boy.

27. ☐ He had conflicts at work.

28. ☐ He had difficulty keeping a job.

I'm sure you could add something to this list that you have experienced.

Chapter 4

WHY DID I STAY WITH HIM?

Y ou may be asking "Why did I overlook the warning signs?" The short answer is what you needed from him was greater than the reality of who he was. The shorter answer is you did not want to overlook the warning signs.

With rare exception most every girl I've worked with said they saw the problems that he had but it just didn't matter! One young lady told me that after a breakup "I was so mad at myself for not admitting his faults sooner!"

How many of the following were (are) true of you? You stayed with him because ...

1. ☐ I got a high out of the chase. It became a game and I didn't want to lose.
2. ☐ I received attention from him and others.
3. ☐ I wanted my sex/affection needs met.
4. ☐ I valued cuddling/affection more than sex.
5. ☐ I was avoiding being rejected.
6. ☐ I was just like him.
7. ☐ I lacked self-value so I allowed him to treat me anyway he wanted to.
8. ☐ I was being put down or compared to my siblings so I wanted it to work.

9. ☐ I saw a dreamer and that appealed to me.
10. ☐ I saw what I wanted him to be,
       not what he was.
11. ☐ I was never taught what a good
       relationship should be like.
12. ☐ I was not taught how to recognize
       a bad relationship.

Your reason may not be listed here. You may not clearly understand why you stayed with him. It may take talking to someone to help you figure that out. Actually, it's not always necessary to know *why* you stayed in a bad relationship. But what is necessary is that you learn from what you overlooked and to not make the same mistake again.

PART TWO

The Stories of
Three Girls
In Their Own Words

Author's Note

These young ladies will now share their story in their own words. Each one had a toxic relationship as discussed in this book at various levels. Each story does not have all the elements that other girls experienced but the three stories represent what many have gone through.

There are other stories that contain extreme behavior from girls I've worked with but they did not want to relive the pain by sharing their experience. The kind of experiences they had, however, are mentioned in these first chapters.

It was while working with many young ladies that I found the inspiration to write about their experiences. Each story is different yet similar. Each one struggled with *why* this happened to them and each one reached out for answers.

The desire of each girl in sharing their story is to help others that are involved in a similar relationship; you are not alone!

Chapter 5

NICOLE'S STORY

I first met Nicole when she was twenty-three. As soon as she sat down she said, "I'm going crazy!" She was somewhat joking but actually more serious than not. She quickly explained how her thoughts and feelings were overwhelming her because of past relationships. She really thought something was terribly wrong with her.

Nicole is attractive and very talented. She plays the guitar, sings (great voice), writes poetry, and is a creative writer as you shall see. The following is her story, in her own words, in response to questions over many months.

Discuss your family background.

I was raised by my mom – she's strong and incredibly independent, but she didn't have the best childhood growing up. Her mother was unkind to her and verbally and physically abusive towards her (I saw her hit my mom first-hand). Unfortunately my mom didn't have any other example of what a mother should be, or healed from past experiences from her own life, so some of those behaviors were carried on to her children.

How did she treat you? She's quick to point out flaws, mistakes – slow to acknowledge accomplishments and good traits. On the contrary, she can also be very kind and loves quality time with my sister and I.

The problem, however, is that I very much crave my own life and independence. I've never been respected as an adult in my mother's eyes.

I've always been a child, no matter how old, and even when I was out of her house both times. The best my mom and I got along was actually the second time I moved out and I felt like I could provide more for myself, and I feel like maybe there was a small time-frame when maybe she did see me as an adult.

Now that I'm back in her house, that's all changed and it's back to pointing out what I'm doing wrong, what I haven't done, what's a mess, what I need to do to get my life together (simultaneously paired with how she "doesn't care" what I do as long as I'm happy).

How has it been? It's been very up and down and I feel like my mom and I live in these extremes. We either get along really, really well when I make sure I make enough time for her in my life, or we butt heads whenever she feels like she's being neglected as a mother and a person. It's a very hard battle that I still struggle with to this day, unfortunately. It's upsetting because my mom deserves so much good – but she isolates herself to keep from getting hurt. She's bitter against those who have hurt her and the resentment is deeply rooted and she has to let it out one way or another.

I have a half-sister. She's 18 years old and the first love of my life. She's been the reason I haven't given up a lot of the times that I've wanted to.

I was raised by my half-sister's dad as well from the ages of 7 until just about two years ago when him and I had a falling out. He was the closest and only father figure I've had in my life.

My mom has been the one to provide for my sister and I and I feel like that's been such a burden on her. She's never tried to do things for her own happiness but instead for me and my sister's well-being.

Was there divorce in your family?

My mom was married once and divorced. I was very young and don't remember very much of that relationship, partly because I lived with my grandmother and aunt (mom's little sister) when I was a child and wasn't very involved in my mother's life at that point in time. I do remember, though, not liking her husband, and I definitely didn't like him with my mom. My mom met my sister's dad when I was about 6 years old. Although they never married, they were together a couple of years and split up after my sister's first birthday. My step-dad moved out but we kept in very close contact with him and I started spending more time with him and his family as well.

What was the relationship with your biological dad like?

There was never a relationship with my biological dad. All I know about him are stories that others have told me. He was a successful and wealthy business man, and I was actually the product of an affair. I saw him once when I was a baby (don't remember any details, I've just been told), and then the last time I saw him was for my 6th birthday when I lived with my grandmother and she got in contact with him to see me for my birthday. I did, and although specific memories and scenes of that day have been forgotten and faded from my memory, I always remember that my 6th birthday was the very last time I saw or heard from my biological dad.

Do you have a relationship with your step parents?

My sister's dad is an incredible man. He's taught me a lot of what I didn't know about what a father figure was supposed to be. He understood my love of Pokémon and video games and I remember being young and riding in his red hatchback sports car and going to Game Stop.

So you always got along with him? I hated him at first because he took the attention my mom had for me off of me, and onto him. It took a very long time for us to understand one another and he realized I was just a young pre-teen with way too many emotions. But he was great; he and his family always welcomed me as his other daughter and nothing less.

Unfortunately about a year and a half ago, maybe two years ago at this point, I moved out of the apartment I shared with my ex–boyfriend and I had gone to my step-dad to see if there was any way I could possibly move into his house with his wife (not my mom). There was some sort of miscommunication, unmet expectations? To this day, I don't know exactly what the root of the problem was, but our relationship has never been the same. We stopped talking entirely, and I had started dating my [current] boyfriend and became less and less involved in trying to make things work and just trying to figure out my own life and what steps I needed to take.

Where did you live? I moved in with my mom and slept on her couch for several months before my sister asked me to just start sleeping in her room like a normal person. My step-dad and his wife both have tried to reach out to me, inviting me to parties and get-togethers at their house but it's always been very last minute, and I couldn't go - which then led to frustration on their end (more specifically and obviously my step-dad) because it just seemed like I was avoiding them or just didn't care to make time for them.

Was that true? In reality, I didn't want to expose myself to another situation where I'd get my feelings hurt. Inevitably, it led to more distance and about 6 months ago I finally decided to go and see my step-dad and apologize to him. It didn't go over well. We have very different ways of communicating and very different personalities. Unfortunately that was the last time I saw him and it's only gotten worse. I miss him, because like I said – he was the only father figure I had and at times the only person I could talk to when my mom was angry with me and isolating herself.

Discuss your family dynamics.

Was there arguing, yelling, fighting, positive or negative feedback, drugs, alcohol, encouragement?

All of the above was/is true..except drugs! My mom and I have the worst dynamic in the house, more so now than ever. My sister tries to avoid conflict and keep the peace, especially between my mom and I when it's tense. Because my mother and I are so similar, we butt heads a lot.

My mom is very quick with her words and very, very quick to place blame on others, point out mistakes and things that she doesn't like or approve of, or makes jokes (putting the others down) to lighten the mood (which honestly just makes it worse and makes me angry). Although she denies it and says that she's perfectly fine, I believe my mom feels very alone and instead of reaching out to us, she isolates herself from my sister and I and desperately wants US to be the ones to reach out to her because it shows her that we care. When in reality, when she shuts down, she's actually pushing us away.

The phase of my life that I'm currently in pertaining to my family is probably the most difficult I've ever faced. My sister is 18 and in college and is finding her independence, and goes out with friends a lot more, and also spends a lot of time with her dad and his side of the family. This causes my mom to feel rejected, alone, and angry. Angry towards my sister and accuses her of choosing her "other family" over her "real family" which puts a lot of unneeded pressure on my little sister and causes me to really have to bite my tongue. Sometimes I do speak my mind, which turns our house into a battlefield. I don't like people being unfair and unkind, and especially when it comes to those I love. I love my mom, she's the strongest and most independent woman I know – but to a fault.

Growing up, my mom I think was more focused on providing for us than actually being emotionally available for us. My sister has her dad, but I really didn't have anyone to go to aside from my mom. I'd go to her for words of confirmation, or to confide in her about my troubles and insecurities. And then by the next time we were fighting, she'd be using my own words against me. Either to mock me or make fun of me or to throw in my face why my life was working out the way it was.

How did you handle all of that? I was sleeping around because I was trying to fill a void? I was a slut. It was already difficult growing up with horrible insecurities and the words from someone I was supposed to look up to became words that were planted from the get-go and became my way of living life and seeing myself. There have been so many moments in my life where I've had to really choose my battles.

Between trying to make my mom realize what she said or did was hurtful, or just biting my tongue and taking jab after jab. Sometimes I was even the one to go and apologize just so my mom would talk to me again.

I've been called names by my mom when she was angry, I've been told I'm lazy, dirty, nasty. Those aren't exactly the words you want at the very back of your head as a child – or ever. At one point in time, early/mid-teens, my mom's way of dealing with my horrible attitude and quick-tongue was to hit me. In the middle of the store across my mouth/face, pulling my hair whenever I was acting up at home, calling me names and once even telling me to "go to hell" when we got into an argument.

These things were normal to me. It became what I thought was what I deserved, and well – my biological dad didn't want me anyway, and I didn't live with my mom for so long, was it because she didn't want me to? These were constant and reoccurring thoughts. I remember one time my mom raised her hand to hit me in the face, and I remember grabbing her arm and the look on her face is something I'll never forget. She started crying and screaming at me, saying I was an ungrateful daughter, a disrespectful daughter. That no child should ever raise their hand towards their parents. I was distraught and confused, and to this day, don't know what happened in her head to make her think that I was the one hitting HER. I didn't. I defended myself because at what point is enough, enough? I wasn't and shouldn't be a punching bag for someone else's lack of healing and happiness. I won't say it's my parents' entire fault, because in reality I still had many choices that only I could make growing up. However, it has shaped a lot of who I am. I apologize for everything and anything. And definitely have apologized just so whoever was on the other end of the conversation would stop insulting or yelling at me. I've never truly felt safe with anyone, I don't think.

What was your opinion of yourself growing up?

I can openly acknowledge now that I had a huge attitude problem growing up. I had a phase where I thought I was untouchable, and I feel like a lot of my rebellion was because I felt so trapped where I was – physically and emotionally. I made horrible mistakes for the sake of filling a void. I have a huge emotional capacity, which unfortunately means that I also have a tendency to wear my emotions on my sleeve.

I was teased a lot and to this day struggle with so much insecurity which has led to me playing the victim game many, many times. I did a lot of attention-seeking things and wanted to feel accepted and loved so I put myself out there a lot emotionally, between friendships and "relationships." Because I never got the attention I wanted from my mom and biological dad, I ended up steering in the wrong direction and headed down a really dangerous and promiscuous road. I started seeking out attention from guys and felt that if I could have a guy like me, maybe then I could get some sort of validation. Maybe at some point in time, I could meet someone who genuinely liked me. Unfortunately, because of my upbringing, I was a doormat. I took every word that was spoken to me and believed it, I believed that the things done to me were because I deserved it – so why would anyone else be any different?

How old were you when you started dating?

I started dating when I was probably 14 or 15. I was incredibly interested in boys from a very young age. I just call that daddy-issues at this point.

Describe the worse dating relationship you've had.

I have had three bad relationships and I can definitely talk about this topic; his name was Shawn.

Shawn

How did you meet Shawn?

We officially met in school when I was in 6th grade and he was in 8th grade.

How long did the relationship last?

Off and on, probably a little bit over a year.

How did he treat you?

When we met, we didn't have anything to do with each other. He was two years older, and in middle school my attention was on something else. We didn't actually connect until right after I graduated high school. He found me on Facebook and we started talking. He was a sweet-talker and very charming and funny. We started dating and shortly after he told me he had enlisted in the military. He told me he'd be more than willing to start a relationship if that's still what I wanted, despite the fact that he'd be gone for two months for basic training. We wrote letters back and forth since that was our only real means of communication (plus one phone call on the weekends at some point), and it was all so real and romantic and everything I thought a relationship should be long distance, of course. We discussed having a life together and how we were going to get married once he was all done. I was proud of him, and I liked his family. They included me in a lot of what they did even while he was gone.

Unfortunately, it all started crumbling the moment I went with his family to his basic training graduation. I had been very guilty of over sharing every emotion and activity on Facebook at the time. Meaning that every time Shawn would send me a letter back, I'd post about how happy I was and how much I loved him and basically every emotion that you'd see and would make you cringe.

So we go to his graduation and that was all great. But the day we left, I remember crying and his mom telling me that her son "wasn't dying" so there wasn't a need to cry about it. I missed him, and seeing him only to leave again and not see him for another many months? Of course I was crying … again, I wear my emotions on my sleeve. And up to this point I felt comfortable talking to his family and just felt comfortable with them in general. Not after that horrible weekend, though.

Once in the car and on the drive back, I was laughing and watching YouTube videos with his nephew and the mom and Shawn's older sister turn to me and said something along the lines of, "sure seems funny that you were crying just a couple hours ago and now you're laughing. That's pretty two-faced, don't you think?" I was shocked. I felt so completely uncomfortable and trapped, literally. I was in a car with his family with no other way to get back home for the next few hours. I didn't say anything! How could I actually respond to a question like that?

After that, it was very obvious that his family would always take precedence over anything I would ever say or do. Nothing I said or did was good enough, and his family completely turned their backs on me, saying that I wasn't good for him, that I was two-faced, and that I was shoving it in their face on Facebook any time I posted anything about getting a letter from Shawn while he was at basic. They'd say how disrespectful I was and how he should move on without me. I hadn't done anything wrong, and yet Shawn was siding with them every time. And it wasn't one of those situations where he'd try and diffuse the situation, he'd just flat out agree with them. And this whole time we're still apart so it's not making it any easier. The important key note in all of this is that before this he had lived with his mom. He had never experienced freedom and independence. When he did get some freedom, he stayed out late and would go home completely drunk.

So I started getting phone calls late at night. He was drunk and at some club. And then it got worse because the phone calls turned into updates on which girl he'd given his number to. And THEN the phone calls got aggressive and even more upsetting. One night in particular he told me that I was never going to love him as much as his mom loves him, which made absolutely no sense to me. And then it turned into how I don't love him at all – again, it made no sense. But regardless, I stuck it out thinking that this was just a phase and he was enjoying all of his new freedoms and experiences – even the ones that included other girls. These phone calls soon turned into screaming matches, where I'd end uphe told me that I was never going to love him as much as his mom loves him, which made absolutely no sense to me. And then it turned into how I don't love him at all – again, it made no sense. But regardless, I stuck it out thinking that this was just a phase and he was enjoying all of his new freedoms and experiences – even the ones that included other girls. These phone calls soon turned into screaming matches, where I'd end up crying and he'd end up laughing. He continued to brag about all the girls he danced with or gave his number to, all the while I was crying on the other end. I knew I deserved better, but wasn't sure if I'd ever find it. His behaviors and what I assume were his guilty conscience, led to his own suspicions of me cheating on him. Honestly, this just proved time and time again how warped his thinking process was. Regardless, I stayed with him.

When we were together (I spent my paychecks visiting him as much as I could, sometimes once or twice every month), it was completely different. He was loving and affectionate and didn't treat me the way he did over the phone. He wasn't really mean, and he'd make sure to spend time with me when I needed it. But then again, I was at his beck and call and he totally knew it. I was always the one making the drive to go and see him, no matter what the time was or if I had other plans. No one else existed to me in that time frame. I lost all of my friends, my sister and I were constantly fighting, my mom was getting exhausted by my behavior and recognized just how much I was doing and just how much it didn't add up. I truly wasn't getting anything in return. I'd cry almost every day. It wasn't even the distance that bothered me anymore, it was how obvious he made it how much he was distancing himself emotionally and finding company in other women – and then bragging to me about it. He was the youngest of three, being the only boy. His mom was a single mother, who was (I was told by her own family) abused and cheated on by her ex-husband and father to her three kids. Because they were from a small town, everyone knew his dad was no good and that he went around with any woman he found, proudly. That's all I was really told, but this information will tie in later with my relationship with Shawn.

What did he do to you?

The lowest point in my life and worst moment in this relationship was when I went to visit him for the very last time. I remember we stayed at a nice hotel and we were watching TV together. He was lying back with his legs apart while I leaned my back up against him and had my laptop in my lap checking my Facebook. I'll never forget how quick he was to shove me off of him when he saw I had an unread message. He asked me to open it in front of him and asked me multiple times who it was from. Shawn got incredibly angry, angrier than I had ever seen him. He quickly pushed me off the bed and grabbed me by my throat and held me up against the wall. He called me every name you could imagine, a slut, a whore, a fake bitch, all the while he spit in my face accusing me of cheating on him. I wasn't. I had been confiding in my childhood friend who happened to be a guy – Shawn was threatened and angry.

All it took was one unread message to release every ounce of insecurity he had ever felt, I guess. My denial in doing anything set him off even more. He went and grabbed every letter I ever wrote him during his time at basic and started ripping them up in front of me, saying he never loved me, how he deserves more. Realistically, I could have been saying the same thing. I was powerless, defenseless, friendless, and completely alone, miles away from home and safety.

I made the trip to San Antonio that weekend by myself and took a bus there. I had just gotten into a horrible fight with my best friend at the time because she hated Shawn and warned me before I left. My mom was sad and tired of watching me go out of my way every time and spend the little money I made on going to visit someone who never even lifted a finger to help me in any way. I was completely alone and had no one to call and no one to blame but myself. I was too scared to call the police in that moment, but looking back I should have.

As every thought was rushing through my head and I could feel my tears streaming down my face, he once again picked me up by my arms and threw me on the bed and started choking me again. As he had both hands around my throat, I completely went blank and accepted that I deserved all of this. I stopped crying and just stared up at him as he kept spewing venom through his lips. I'll never forget the words he said as he looked at me and told me, "you know the difference between my dad and I? He didn't kill my mom, but I could kill you, right now."

I don't remember what happened between him saying that and me sitting back up. He was still angry as I sat up in the bed, and he was pacing back and forth and packing his belongings as I stared, numb. He went towards the door and something inside of me possessed me to sprint towards the door and block him from leaving, asking him to please stay and calm down. I didn't want to cause a scene, and at that moment he was about to cause an even bigger one. After much back and forth and yelling (I'm surprised no one ever called the police, honestly), he left and I was alone in the hotel room. I couldn't figure out what to do, who to call, and if I should even tell anyone anything. I called my mom crying and didn't tell her what happened, but asked if she could please come and pick me up because the next available bus didn't leave until the next morning. I had no way out, and because she was still upset, she had told me that I was an adult and made my choice. I couldn't tell her what happened; I knew she'd call the police and I was terrified of what could happen in between that time.

Shawn finally came back several minutes later, stumbling through the door. He didn't say a word to me but he had drank his way through a six-pack of beer he got at the gas station down the road. He was laughing in my face moments later, threatening to post some status on his Facebook about how big of a whore I am and change our relationship status online. I let him say whatever he wanted; I just didn't want him to touch me again. I was terrified of him, of what he told me and how true it was. He tried walking towards me and I flinched, which made him laugh even harder. He plopped himself onto the bed as I just stood on the side and watched what he'd do next. He started building a wall of pillows next to him joking about how that's how we were going to sleep for the rest of our lives. I couldn't believe the words he was saying. He'd lost his mind. Or maybe this was the first time I was seeing things clearly, who knows. An hour passed and I was exhausted and sitting on the floor. I tried grabbing some pillows to take into the bathroom and hoped to sleep in there and lock the door and block out all the nightmares I didn't realize were yet to come. He didn't let me. He grabbed me again and forced me onto the bed with him, laughing and calling me a whore, telling me how what he was doing to me was what I wanted from the other guy anyway. That's when I started screaming and crying, begging him to let me go. He started undressing me while he kept laughing. I kept saying "no" over and over again but it didn't matter at that point; it was too late and he was stronger than I was. I cried the entire time until he finished and rolled over and passed out. I don't think I'd ever felt as worthless as I did in that moment. I wanted to die. I wish he would have killed me, I thought. I was shaking uncontrollably. When I woke up, he was already awake and getting dressed. He saw me and smiled the same familiar smile I had grown to love, and I knew it – he didn't care, or he didn't remember. This was just another day to him. He came over to hug me and I froze up, completely paralyzed by the realization. I had bruises all over my neck and arms and I followed his gaze as he noticed every single one, grazing his fingers lightly over them. He started kissing each bruise and telling me he was sorry and I honestly felt so sick to my stomach. I wanted to hurt him as badly as he had hurt me, but all I could do was collapse and cry. I wanted to go home and never see or hear from him again. I left that weekend and sad to say, I didn't stick to that plan. He asked for forgiveness countless times and said he'd never lay a hand on me again or make me do anything I didn't want to do. But it was far too late at that point to ever trust him again.

I went back home and he went back to his drunk texts and calls. Eventually he confessed to sleeping with the girl he always called his best friend. What was worse is that she knew about me. She knew he had a girlfriend. She was the only friend I didn't get to meet every time I saw him - shocking, right? I found out the truth little by little. Once it was confirmed and he admitted to it (sober), I left him. I may not have thought very highly of myself, or deserving of much else, but I knew I deserved a hell of a lot more than that. He ended up marrying that girl, and I haven't spoken to him since.

Did you live with him?

This was one of my biggest mistakes in this relationship. Moving in with someone as quickly as I did was already foolish, moving in with someone who had already disrespected me and still thinking it would turn out okay, was worse. I moved in with him after about 6 months of being together

Did you have thoughts of suicide?

I definitely wanted to die after he raped me, that was the lowest I've ever felt. I didn't try, although I did have a few occasions where I'd cut myself (my thighs so no one could see). But I think deep down I didn't want to die. I just wanted to feel something again.

Were you ever in a mental hospital?

No. I was never admitted to a mental hospital.

Were you ever put on medication?

No, never.

What did he want you to do?

The main thing that sticks out now is just not hanging out or having any sort of relationship with anyone who was a guy. Looking back, I lost a lot of friends and it was incredibly toxic and controlling behavior.

What were you thinking during the relationship?

I think there were several moments when I told myself, maybe if I do this, he'll stay. Maybe if I do this, he'll love me and respect me. I think I was willing to do anything to make sure the relationship worked, even if it meant losing myself in the process.

What did you do to keep the relationship?

I spent every check I got basically to go and visit him. Whether it was flying or taking a bus, and then the hotel itself was always something I paid for. It was never a mutual agreement; it was just the way it was. He knew I was willing to do whatever, and he didn't even have to ask because I was always one step ahead of him. Financially, I was the one contributing more to the relationship, emotionally as well, though. I was fully emotionally invested in him and the thing was, he knew that and took advantage of it. I worked out almost every single day and tried to be incredibly health conscious and became obsessed with counting calories. I lost a ton of weight and looked great; I was toned and tiny and the smallest weight I'd been and I figured he'd never leave me for another girl. How could he, right?

What did your family and friends tell you to do?

They got tired of trying to talk to me about the relationship; I just wasn't budging. They all knew he was a bad decision and I didn't listen and made so many excuses as to why he behaved the way he did. I put a lot of the blame on myself, if not all of it. I lost my best friend at the time, and my mom and I drifted apart more than we ever had before. They all tried to get me to come back to earth and realize what kind of person he was, and how it didn't match up with the person I was.

Did you see warning signs? Did you ignore them? Why?

Absolutely. Him siding with his family and not defending me when I hadn't done anything wrong was where it started. Then it was the drunk phone calls and his behavior with other women and him being so unashamed and open about it to me. He completely disrespected me and the relationship the moment he left his mother's house. I ignored it and came up with excuses as to why he was acting that way.

I figured he needed to get some things out of his system since he was on his own for the very first time. I blamed myself and my insecurities got worse because I realized maybe I wasn't enough for him, but we were both too stupid to leave each other, and well – if he wasn't going to budge, neither was I. There was a lot of pride in the process, as well as just denial.

How did the relationship end?

I guess you could say I "officially" ended it. But he broke us the moment he got involved with another person, the moment he emotionally distanced himself, and the moment he started disrespecting me. It was over way before it was actually over and I walked away. I figured if I didn't leave, I'd probably end up dead or killing myself trying to make it work.

Did you try to get him back?

Him and I had split up for maybe a day or two once during his drunk call sessions, but it was easy and mutual to get back together. I think in some twisted way, we liked hurting each other and romanticized the making up as if what happened the night before wasn't a big deal. I definitely broke things off the moment I realized he had been having a relationship with his other "friend". There was no way I was going to be a second option, ever.

Did you get others to help you get him back?

No, it was just me, myself, and I.

Did you try to hurt him?

I considered calling the police for a very, very long time but couldn't bring myself to do it. I'm sure he would have lost his job. But I decided that he wasn't worth any more of my time, and I had a lot of repairing that I needed to do within myself. I was physically and emotionally exhausted and numb for months.

How did you bring closure?

The hard way. It was a traumatic experience and only then did I see where that relationship would have led me.

How long did it take?

It took me several years. Even now there are moments when I have a lot of doubts and have difficult moments where I think my current boyfriend deserves more than me, that I'm not good enough, that maybe he's cheating on me. I think a lot of the mess wasn't properly dealt with and there's still traces of it I run into every now and then.

Identify the person that helped you change your thinking. Did you go to therapy?

Yes, it was you!! ☺ (Unfortunately just a few years too late.)

Did it help?

Yes, and still does!

What did you learn in therapy?

It's helped me realize that my worth is much, much, much more than I ever realized – no matter the mistakes I've made. We're all human, we all mess up and will fall down and stumble, but it's the things we learn along the way and what we take out of those experiences.

I also learned that there are guys out there that will take advantage of my kindness and good heart.

Would you go back to him?

No. That time is done and it's going to stay that way. I learned a lot, I wish him the best, but it's my time to be happy and do the things that I love. I needed to learn to love myself a long time ago.

What did you learn?

I regret not leaving when I knew I should have – the moment he didn't stick up for me I realized he'd never respect me as anything but a plaything.

What would you have done differently? I probably would have and should have never pursued anything after he left for basic training, honestly. I became borderline obsessive and possessive and that just isn't me. I have had to and am STILL having to unlearn so many behaviors I picked up during that time of my life.

I was trying so hard to fill a void because I felt like my parents never really loved me enough or gave me the attention I needed so I went to any person who gave it to me and would latch onto them for dear life thinking that they could be the answer. Spoiler alert: they definitely were not.

Are you in a healthy relationship now?

I've been in a loving, committed, and healthy relationship for two years now, and couldn't be more thankful. I know that there were so many experiences and lessons I had to learn to be able to appreciate where I am now. I know now that love isn't manipulative, it isn't guilt-tripping or lying for the sake of "protecting" the other person's feelings. I feel safe and comfortable, and at the end of the day, my boyfriend is also my friend. We are intentional about our communication and when something hurts my feelings, I'm not afraid to tell him that. There were so many moments in my past relationships where I felt trapped or alone, but it shouldn't be that way. The person that you choose to love should love and respect you. And although I'm still learning how to be vulnerable with my boyfriend, I've gotten so much better and it is so freeing to be with someone who respects you and loves you for who you are. Being with someone who wants the best for me and doesn't have a secret agenda has been one of the biggest blessings of my life. Everyone deserves a love they feel safe and 100% themselves in. You deserve to feel beautiful and know that you're wanted and desired in the best way. You deserve someone who motivates you and doesn't kick you when you're already down.

Looking back at my past relationships sometimes stings, even now. But I know that because of a lot of those experiences, I can appreciate what I have now so much more. I never thought I'd be deserving of someone who truly loves me for me ... but it does exist, and I'm so thankful for every moment that led me to where I am now.

What would you want the readers of your story to learn from your experience?

As cliche as it may sound, trust your instincts. Don't excuse things you know are not okay or not normal. There were so many times where there were red flags, and I've had friends see red flags, but deep down, I wanted to be the one to fix him and maybe then he'd love me.

It almost NEVER works that way. You have to be with someone who #1 – RESPECTS you, and genuinely cares for you. Bottom line is, don't cut yourself short. What you think you deserve is probably a lot less than what you ACTUALLY deserve. Know that you're worth loving and worth cherishing. Learn to love yourself first before you try to love anyone else. Don't try to make up for the self-love deficit.

Update To Nicole's Story

Nicole married her boyfriend eight months after writing her story and told me "It's been a long journey but I'm the happiest I've ever been; healthier, emotionally, and mentally." She then said " I'm a lucky woman. He brings out the best in me and we're a good team."

Chapter 6

MADDY'S STORY

I will never forget the first time I met Maddy. She entered the room like a lightning bolt that suddenly changes the darkness into light! So vivacious, charming, winsome, and full of energy and life!

To say she has a wonderful soft heart is to not do her justice, she is an extremely tenderhearted, caring, very attractive, bright young lady. She sings, dances, and she too is a creative writer as you will see. She loves animals and being outdoors.

As her story began to unfold, it was obvious she had experienced as bad a relationship as I had ever heard. Her story will break your heart as it did mine. She had been abused for a long period of time and now she was confused and felt overwhelmed. Maddy thought she was none of those things mentioned above.

Before we started discussing her experience she told me "Telling my story will probably be the hardest thing I've ever done. Talking about your feelings is never an easy task. Especially when it was a time when you were the weakest and most vulnerable that you've ever been."

The following is her story, in her own words, in response to my questions. She was twenty-one years old at the writing of her story.

Discuss your family dynamics.

Was there arguing, yelling, fighting, positive or negative feedback, drugs, alcohol, encouragement in the family? Parents ever divorced?

First, my parents have never been divorced. They have been married twenty-five years. There were all of those things you just mentioned. They argued and yelled at us and each other a lot. I had some positive feedback but also a lot of negative feedback.

Any drug or alcohol use/abuse? There were no drugs used in my home but there was alcohol used mainly by my mom.

Was I encouraged? Looking back now, not really because I was treated like there was something not right about me. I was not like my sisters. I had some positive feedback but also a lot of negative feedback mostly from my sisters.

Tell me about your father.

My dad grew up in a small town and had been adopted. He did not have siblings in his adopted family. He did not meet his birth parents until he was thirty years old and then found out he had a brother and sister. My dad is very sarcastic so I did not quite understand his humor. He is very laid back and chilled. He worked full time.

How did that affect you growing up? Well, I can now see how that affected me a lot. I had it in my head that there was something wrong with me and him being sarcastic kind of said to me that there *was* something wrong with me or he would not have said treated me the way he did. It was confusing at times. Was he serious or not? I didn't know for sure so I thought he was.

Tell me about your mother.

Mom grew up on a farm in a small rural town in the mid-west. She has three sisters. Her dad died when she was seven from throat cancer. My mom and her sisters had to take care of the farm by themselves. Mom is a very anxious person. She gets nervous over little things.

Mom gave me a lot of attention growing up because I had a lot of issues with how I acted. Ever since the age of 10 I was told that I was"different" and that something was wrong with me.

My mom is not like my dad, she is over anxious and loud. She worked part time and so she was basically a stay at home mom.

Tell me about your grandparents.

I didn't have much of a relationship with my grand parents because they lived far away. My Nana and Papa lived about six hours away. My other Grandpa and Grandma lived in another state which is a ten hour drive.

Tell me about your siblings.

I have two siblings, both girls, actually we are triplets. We were born minutes apart. We all came out within five minutes, I was the last so I'm the youngest by about two minutes! Can you believe that! Two minutes!

Did you and your sisters get along with each other?

Not even! We fought like cats and dogs! There was a lot of yelling and screaming between us. There was hair pulling, kicking, and biting! We were also constantly compared to each other by other people and ourselves. I always came up on the short end.

My five minute older sister (!) didn't like me so we fought the most. Since I was so different from my sisters our mom gave me a lot of attention. That made my older sister feel rejected and so she took it out on me. I was also good at sports and that made my sisters jealous of me.

How were you different from your sisters? I had a lot of energy so I was very active and really liked being outside and playing sports. I was always on the move and way more active than my sisters were, I just couldn't sit still!

I also liked being alone but I was told that was not okay either. I got irritated when I did not get some time to myself but again I was told that was not okay. Can you see how confused I was growing up?

Author's note: Maddy has the natural ability to get very excited and is very playful. She is so fun to talk to. She laughs, smiles, and has a huge capacity to enjoy life. Because she was so excitable and impulsive she was told that it wasn't normal and that something was wrong with her. She has been on/off medication since the age of ten which blunts her emotions and takes from her who she really is ... a fun loving, excitable young lady.

Tell me some things that happened growing up since you were treated like something was wrong with you.

First, what was your opinion of yourself growing up? Not very good. I actually had a pretty low opinion of myself growing up. I grew up with a lot of insecurities because of being compared to my sisters and being criticized. I was very insecure with my body and felt that I was not beautiful. I would always walk with my head down, eyes downcast, and shoulders hunched over.

I've been told by lots of people that I have a really tender heart. That's probably why I wanted everybody to like me. It so bothers me when someone is upset with me. I think that's why I give guys what they want so they will like me. When I think a guy is upset with me I give him more...well, you know what I mean? *Yes I do.*

When were you put on medication? Ever since the age of ten (even before) I was told that I was "different" and that something was wrong with me. I was told that I had ADHD [Attention Deficit Hyperactivity Disorder] and was put on medication then. One of my teachers told me I was stupid!

What! Oh my! Yeah, and I believed her because I had been told something was wrong with me all my life. I really did believe that there was something wrong with me because I was not like my sisters.

When I was in the fourth grade I left one my books at school ... I just forget. My mom and sisters flipped out. You would have thought I had burned down the school!

When I was in the seventh grade I started to pull out my hair because of my anxiety and low self-esteem. It got so bad that people began to notice. There's a thin spot right here [pointing to her hair line on the   upper left side] and my hair will not grow back.

When I went through puberty I changed a lot. They had to change my meds because I cried a lot for no particular reason. Looking back, I was trying to figure out who I was and was very confused. I wanted to be active (I loved running) and play sports, and have fun ... lots of fun! But it was not okay.

Did someone tell you it wasn't okay to do those things? Well, yeah, it was my parents. On those medications I was, well, numb! The meds caused muscle tension and it affected me playing sports. I lost my energy being on those meds.

Are you still on meds? Yeah, they help me concentrate now that I'm in college. But as soon as I'm no longer in school, I'm going to stop taking them!

Didn't you tell me once before that you were bullied? Yeah, I was. One time, in the sixth grade, my friends turned on me and stole some things out of my back pack. I was made fun of too. I was bullied while playing sports too.

Why were you bullied? Looking back I think I had so much energy that no one took me seriously. I wanted everyone to like me so other kids found it easy to pick on me. I didn't fight back. I did with my sisters but not with others.

Can you give me an example of what happened? Yeah. The worst thing one girl did to me was when she picked up a piece of gum from the floor, re-wrapped it, and put it back in the pack! This girl then turned to me and asked "Hey Maddy! Do you want some gum?" Without even thinking about it I said "Sure" and popped in my mouth. I then proceeded to spit out the piece of gum after crunching on a piece of dirt while she and her friends began to laugh at me hysterically! I was only sixteen years old and I didn't have the courage or strength to fight back.

How old were you when you started dating?

I was seventeen. It was during the summer before my senior year of high school.

Tell me about your first boyfriend.

I met a boy named Lorenzo. He was a different kind of boy then I was used to being around. I became completely obsessed with him.

Growing up as a young woman in an upper middle class family I was expected to date someone who was well put together and had a future plan in life. This guy was everything but any of that. He had been charged with aggravated assault and faced a possible prison sentence. He drank on an almost daily basis and took all kinds of drugs.

Tell me about his personality? It would take him two hours to get ready to go outside. It took me about forty-five minutes! He was so picky about how he looked. He would never let me touch his hair!

His lifestyle appealed to you? Yeah, and it scared me too. He knew a world that I had never seen, parties, alcohol, sleeping around with different people. I could only imagine what that was like. It was all so exciting to me yet so very frightening.

I didn't even drink until my prom night of my senior year. One of the first times I ever hung out with him alone we sat at his house drinking a handle of vodka as we debated what movie we were going to go see. When I came home that night my sister was so mad that she told our parents and I was grounded for the next two weeks.

Never before had I been the rebellious sort of girl. I always aimed to please my parents and live up to their expectations. So much was expected of me from my parents, I felt smothered. I could not be myself. I was criticized, compared to my sisters by my parents and others. But after a lifetime of doing so, I was fed up. Suddenly I didn't care what they thought and instead I just wanted to spite them.

How did he treat you?

He would always belittle me. All the time he would get irritated over the slightest little thing I did. He would never listen to me! He just would not let me express my feelings and let me cry.

He was an alcoholic and a drug addict; he did coke, drank half a handle by himself. He used me for his pleasure and then cheated on me all of the time. I ignored it.

Why did you tolerate his behavior? He was my first, well you know, and I really cared for him. I loved him and thought he would change and stop doing those things to me.

One night when we went out to a party together he got super drunk. He was about to get sick and he wanted me to take him home. On the ride back he threw up all in my car, on the side, and on himself. When we got there he could not even walk! I had to help him get into his home. I had to take off his clothes and give him a shower. I got him dressed, put him to bed, laid him on his side, and tucked him in. The next day he did not even muster a word of thanks! He didn't help me clean up the mess he left in my car.

He wrecked my car. I let him borrow my car to get breakfast. He popped a curb and ripped my tire to shreds as well as scratched the crap out of my tire rim! When I told him that he needed to pay for it he looked me dead in the eye and told me that I did not deserve the money!

Another time we went to my friend's party and drank too much. The party was on my street so we planned to walk to my house afterwards and go to bed. On the walk back to my house he decided that he wanted to go home. I said "No, the plan was to stay at my house! Neither one of us are able to drive right now!" He said "No! I need to go home and sleep in my own bed! I'll just take your car and drive home!" So we kept going back and forth and arguing until I realized he really was going to leave with my car with or without me. So I went with him and went to his house and within thirty minutes he told me I was too loud and needed to leave!

I just started crying and told him I couldn't even drive my car! I wasn't supposed to be there anyway. I just couldn't stop crying and sobbing. I just gave up and slept on the floor.

One of the most hurtful things he did was he showed no empathy when my dog died. He was really sick and I had to put him down. He did not care and just went to work. He didn't call his job to see if he could get off ... he just didn't care. I loved my dog and I just wanted him to be with me and show some emotion. It just wasn't in him to do that. I just wanted to be held and told that everything was going to be okay. Instead, he left me alone with my dog.

What were you thinking when things like that would happen? I just wanted him to care about me like I cared for him. I thought he would change one day ... I was wrong. I lied to myself.

All my life I've wanted everybody to like me and I didn't want to be rejected so I tolerated a lot just so no one would be upset with me.

Did you live with him?

Well you might say I did. He lived at home with his mom and I stayed there a lot overnight.

His mother was okay with that? Yeah, she liked me but he didn't let me spend much time with her.

Did he abuse you sexually?

This is hard to talk about but yes, he did! He pressured me to have sex with him all the time two and three times a day. He choked me one time during it and I almost passed out. He would also pressure me to have sex with him when it was too risky. We could have been caught. Once at a party at a friend's house, he pressured me to have sex with him in the bathroom.

Did you give in? Yes I did. But I was really afraid that someone would come in on us. I was so mad at him but I was afraid not to.

He pressured me to have a threesome with me, him, and another girl. But I refused to do that. He was mad about that too.

Did he ever rape you? I think you can say he did. One time I was asleep and I woke up because he was on top on me, and well, you know he was already, uh, engaged. I didn't stop him but it was not what I wanted to do.

What did your friends and family think of him?

All my friends kept telling me he was a bad guy. None of my friends liked him. A few got mad at me because I didn't leave him. He had so many outbursts. I never knew what was going to set him off. They all knew that.

He cheated on me a lot and my friends knew that too. I lied to myself and just ignored what he did.

My family didn't like him either but they didn't know what he was doing to me. I lied to them about most everything about him.

Why didn't you listen to them? I don't know. I guess I really wanted to make it work. I thought I could fix him.

Have you ever thought about harming yourself?

Yea, I thought about it a few times. I never tried. I never got to that point because I knew if I didn't stop thinking about it I would reach the point of no return.

Have you ever been in a mental hospital?

Yea, three times! I was put in one the first time after a guy criticized me in front of my friends and I got so angry at him. I lost it emotionally so they put me in one to get me stable. I was put on more medication.

The second time a guy chose my best friend over me. I lost it emotionally, again! I was so angry and broke a door. I called 911 on myself because I was afraid of what I might do next.

The third time, I was at a party in another city. I went there to see a friend and to just get out of town. Things got a little carried away that night and I had a little too much to drink. I was in the bathtub and thought about drowning myself so I called 911. They took me to a mental hospital but I only stayed there a day.

Were you put on more medication? Not the last time I was in that hospital. I've been on medication since I was around eleven. I don't like that stuff. It makes me feel like a zombie! I can't be myself, I can't feel.

Have you been having panic attacks?

Oh for sure! That's what happened just before I went to the mental hospital every time. Sometimes I would get so upset I was like in a fog. I was so out of control I scared myself.

Did the medication help? It calmed me down and helped to concentrate but I stopped being me.

How did the relationship end?

He broke up with me. But it didn't end there. I had a complete mental breakdown six months after breaking up with him. I was fed up with everything and everyone. I could not understand how life could keep going when I felt so miserable. I wanted everyone around me to feel as awful as I did on the inside. I would scream, cry, and throw temper tantrums! I told my mom and older sister that I hated them almost every day.

I kept seeing him once a month just to give him what he wanted, you know...! I did that once a month every month for about a year. We did miss a few months, so about nine times.

Do you remember when you brought a friend with you to one of our sessions? Yes, a friend of mine said she wanted to meet you so I brought her to one of our sessions. When I left the room to go to the restroom she told you the real reason she came was to tell you that

I was still seeing Lorenzo. When I came back into the room you said my friend had given you permission to talk to me about that.

Do you remember what I said to you? Yes, you asked me why I had not told you about seeing Lorenzo for the last year. I said that I didn't want to disappoint you.

You expected me to be upset? Yeah, I suppose I did. Nobody liked him and everybody wanted me to leave him alone. I figured you would be upset with me if you knew.

Was I upset with you? Oh no! You said that nothing I could ever do would disappoint you. You said you cared for me unconditionally and wanted what was best for me.

Why did you keep seeing him? Honestly, I though if I gave him what he wanted that he would change and come back to me. It didn't work, he just finally stopped calling me. *So the relationship is over?* Oh yes!

It took me two years to get back on my feet mentally. The reason I decided to change was because I was forced to depend on myself more which turned out to be the best.

Did he try to contact you after the breakup? Yes he did. Can I share some texts that I sent him? *Of course.*

Author's note. The following are excerpts from texts messages Maddy sent to Lorenzo after the breakup. He first sent Maddy a text stating that he did not understand why she would not respond to his calls. Maddy responded with a few texts telling him how she felt:

"You brought out a side of me that I hated. You made me angry and crazy because I became emotionally dependent on you."

"I think you hate yourself and to cope, you became a compulsive liar."

"I will go far in life because I'm such an amazing person."

"You never deserved me because you treated me like #@%&!"

I finally realized that I did love you but after you got really bad I couldn't let go because I wanted to help "fix you! My mistake!"

"You are also an alcoholic. Just look up the symptoms and you will see."

"Oh, and emotional abuse is worse than physical abuse. The bruises fade but the mental scars never do."

"I'm scared of you!"

Would you go back to him?

If he called, I would have lunch with him but nothing more. Last I heard he had kidney failure and was on dialysis and probably will be the rest of his life and he's only twenty-one! It all caught up with him and he's paying the price. I also heard that he was back in prison.

Maddy shared some journal entries that show her struggles with her self-identity and boyfriend:

1. Bullied throughout high school because people were jealous and said I sucked at sports (which I didn't). I am smart, I am beautiful, and I am important, okay! If you don't believe in yourself who will?

2. How do I feel today? Nervous, scared, excited to see him yet I will not put up with him being a *@#%. Be strong, be super strong! You know that you still have feelings for him but do not let him get to you at all. You will no longer put up with his BS! You are a changed woman Maddy and you are so strong!

You do not need him anymore, tell him this: When you cheated on me it made me feel like I was ugly and I wasn't enough. I feel like we were just not meant to be. I know I have a high maintenance personality.

I feel you do not care about me because of the way you treat me. Why did you never want me to talk to your family? Was I that unimportant that you knew I was not going to last? I feel like I loved you way more than you ever loved me because you've never treated me right! You did in the beginning but as soon as I got clingy you dropped me like a hot potato and had a bunch of side girls behind my back. Or, maybe I was the side girl that would just never leave you alone?

I am sorry that I never gave you the space you wanted but every time we went on a "break" I would sob hysterically for I don't know how long because I couldn't stand the thought of losing you.

3. As I lay here on my make shift palette sleeping bag, I see and contemplate my life. Why can't I let he who shall not be named go? Why can't I just cut him off? I know the easy answer, I still love him. But I feel it's something more than that. I just hope to have the strength to never let him hurt me again. I am beautiful, I am kind, and I am important. I must never forget that or let anyone else try to put me down or hurt me ever again! P. S. Love yourself!

4. If you had told me five years ago that I would end up dating a felon I would not have believed you. Lorenzo was my first boyfriend. He was a lot of firsts for me. When we first started dating we kept our relationship secret because my sisters did not like him. They did not like the fact that he drank a lot and did drugs or that he had been in trouble for physical assault and robbery. I should have known from the very beginning that this guy was bad news! What was I thinking???

5. I was broken so badly that I feel that I will never be whole again. He stole my heart and broke it in ways that I don't even understand yet.

He calls me crazy ... can you believe that! ... but am I truly crazy? Does crazy mean lashing out at your friends and telling them you have them when you are half asleep? Does being crazy mean that you have to go in and out of mental hospitals for over a month and a half because I can't deal with my own self-harm feelings? Does being crazy mean that I always feel like I can't let go of the one person that has hurt me the most? I don't know the answer to these questions and that's why I keep asking them. Maybe one day I'll find out all the answers to these questions!

Have you been able to get some of your questions answered?

Yes, I have. I decided that I'm not the one that is crazy! I know that I wrote that I might not ever be whole again, but I'm getting there. I'm not sure I ever knew what it meant to be whole but I am feeling better about myself.

What you were thinking during the relationship that kept you with him?

Really, I just did want to be alone. I thought who else would want to take me, who would want to be with me? It never occurred to me that someone would treat me better then I was being treated.

You know, I just wanted to be loved. I really thought if I did everything for him that he would love me.

You really thought that you were not worthy of being loved? You know, I did.

What did you do to keep the relationship?

Well, everything he wanted me to do. I would take him to work and pick him up. I bought drugs for him and alcohol! I didn't talk to anyone about "his business" and lied to my family and friends. The biggest lie was to myself!

What was the lie? That he would change. That if I kept doing everything for him he would love me.

Did your family and friends tell you what you should do?

Everyone that knew us told me it was never going to work. I did not want to believe them. My sisters knew some of the stuff that was happening and they said to leave him.

What warning signs did you see?

He talked to me differently than when we were with other people. In front of others it was better, but when alone he talked down to me. Apparently, I annoyed him on just about everything I did! When I cried (and I did a lot) he would get mad at me and would ask me *why* was I crying?

Whenever he did anything that I thought was wrong, he turned it around on me and made it my fault! So, I had to apologize to him for what he did to me! Could not take responsibility for anything he did to me! It was always my fault! He would try to send me on a guilt trip!

Did he ever assault you? Yes, he did. Once, when he had too much to drink!

Were you injured? It hurt a lot, but my face was red for a while. He only did that once.

Another thing was he took pictures and videos of me and us ... do you know what I mean? (*My response to Maddy, yes I do understand.*) He even took pictures of me while I was asleep and I wasn't wearing anything.

Why did you ignore the warning signs? I really loved him and thought that he would change.

Did you get others to help you get him back?

No.

Did you try to hurt him after the breakup?

No, not physically. My friends wanted to hurt him but I didn't. You might say I tried by telling others the truth about who he really is.

Who would you say he is? A selfish, self-centered person with no conscious. A person who is unable to love anyone but himself! I've learned that he is a narcissist.

What happened that caused you to admit/accept that the relationship was bad?

I just realized that my relationship with him (whom I shall not name) validated what I thought of myself.

And what did you think of yourself? Well, I did not think much of myself because I felt put down and criticized by my family and teachers. I was told that there was something wrong with me. I believe all of them! But when I started seeing that there was nothing wrong with me I realized that he was not building me up but keeping me down. I decided I was better than that!

How long did it take for you to bring closure or have you?

Yes, I have. It took about six months after the breakup.

How did your thinking change during that six months?

I slowly realized that I needed him to say "I'm sorry" but it was not going to happen! I also realized that he never listened to me! I had a point about something and he just didn't care! All I wanted was for him to listen to me!

Who helped you change your thinking.

You helped me understand myself. You taught me that I had a great personality that was emotional and creative. You told me that I had normal feelings and emotions and that I just needed to learn self-control.

Another guy friend showed interest in me and was the opposite of that guy I shall not name! I gained self-confidence.

What did you learn in therapy?

Oh, I learned to respect myself. I've learned coping skills. You taught me how to work through panic attacks ... and I don't have them anymore! I did what you said and put my feet on the floor and put a cold cloth on my forehead. It worked! I also practiced "Adjusting" when things got a little nutty!

You helped me understand myself and to accept myself. You kept telling me that I was normal and that it was okay to have all of that energy. I learned that I deserve to be treated better. I learned that since you believed in me that I should believe in myself.

What do you regret?

A lot! I regret not standing up for myself! I regret not breaking it off sooner! I regret not confronting him with all the lies and the really bad stuff he did to me! He was not a good person and I regret not admitting that to myself sooner. If I had, I would have broken it off much sooner.

What are you looking for in a relationship

Respect! I want someone to listen to me. Let me talk. Let me share my opinion! I want someone that is as sociable as me. I want someone that my family approves of. I want to be able to have a relationship with his parents. Is that asking too much? *My response ... of course not!*

What do you want the readers of your story to learn from your experience?

Don't put up with an abusive relationship. Don't accept being treated with disrespect. Don't accept him cheating on you. Realize that you are worthy and deserve a good relationship.

Wait before getting into another relationship. Give yourself time to heal. Take a break!

Author. Maddy, I would like to thank you for being transparent about your experience. You are truly amazing for enduring so much in your life. You have a lot to offer others and many will benefit from your willingness to share your story and the way you have responded to difficult situations. Be happy and enjoy being you!

Chapter 7

ALLY'S STORY

The first time I met Ally I was impressed with her insightful thinking. She obviously thought deeply about life and her past relationships. She feels deeply and takes life seriously, trying to figure out the cause and meaning of events. She is a very attractive, tall blonde with a certain command about her presence in a room. She is not only bright but also creative. She draws and writes and is a very creative thinker.

We have spent countless hours talking about her life events trying to make sense of them. She is working toward becoming a therapist, and will be terrific in the field. The following is her story, in her own words in response to my questions:

Discuss your family background.

Was there arguing, yelling, fighting, positive or negative feedback, drugs, alcohol, encouragement?

My parents have been married thirty-five years. I was raised in a middle class home. Both my parents worked very hard and have had good jobs for many years.

My parents did argue but most always kept it behind closed doors so I didn't hear much of that growing up. Both drank on occasion but never to excess that I can remember.

I've always been close to my mom and now that I'm grown, I consider her my best friend. We have always talked a lot about everything especially the things I struggled with growing up. My mom has always accepted me for who I am. She understood as I struggled with my own sexuality. My curiosity started when I was really young and at time I was confused about what direction my sexuality would take me.

My dad and I did not connect very well when I was growing up. We were too much alike so we clashed over a lot of things. As I got older we found some common ground in sports. I was pretty athletic and so he became more interest in me because of sports.

He has become more tolerant and understanding of me and my struggles now that I'm older and moved out of the house.

Do you have siblings?

Yes, two sisters. They are about a year and a half older than me. They were a challenge to raise because they had special needs. My parents had to put a lot of effort into raising them so it took a lot of their time. I understood early in my life what they needed to do for my sisters and the sacrifices they had to make.

How did that impact you ? Well, frankly, I felt neglected growing up because of my sister's needs. I understood what my parents had to do so I didn't blame them. My sisters could not take care of themselves so they had to do it all. When I was old enough I started taking care of them myself.

I didn't realize it at the time, but looking back, I think that is why I second guess myself.

Explain that a little more. Well, I had to figure out a lot of stuff on my own so I wasn't sure if I was right or not.

Author's note: During the writing of Ally's story one of her twin sisters suddenly passed away. She was twenty-five.

What was your opinion of yourself growing up?

That's a hard one to answer. I was always serious minded and driven to be independent. I wanted to make my own decisions but doubted myself like I said before. I think you can say I was a very curious person so I asked a lot of questions. I was confused about being attracted to other girls before I had my first boyfriend.

How did you meet your first boyfriend?

I first met Dillon when I was fifteen and a freshman in school. He was two years older than me.

Did you start a dating relationship at that age? Yes, he was the first guy I dated. Actually, he was the first one with whom I became sexually active.

Did you parents know you were sexually active at that age? Yeah, my dad actually saw us one evening in the car as he was pulling up to the house. It was a full moon and he saw enough to know what we were doing! *Did you get in trouble?* Yeah, a little!

Discuss the relationship with your boyfriend.

It started off great. The first year and a half he treated me really well. But after he graduated high school he changed. He joined the military and came back after three months from being in boot camp. He was a totally different guy!

How so? Well, he was full of hate toward certain groups of people. I ignored it as much as I could but it kept getting worse. He even hated his parents, especially his mother. He told me once that she gave him a drug that knocked him out!

Did he show anger toward you? Oh yeah! He became verbally and physically abusive to me! He wanted to control everything I did. He was so private about his *business* as he called it. He didn't want me telling anybody anything about him or us.

All my friends did not like him and everybody kept telling me to leave him. I didn't know how to do that I was so scared.

He started every argument we ever had, 100% of them! He intimidated me because of his size, and he used it against me! He would shove me and push me around. One big argument we got into (don't remember what it was about but it never took much) ended with him running toward a moving car! He wanted to die I guess. I pulled him out of the way at the last second or he would have been killed. After that I thought I could never leave him because if I did he would kill himself. I felt responsible.

Did he sexually abuse you? Oh yeah! He forced himself on me numerous times and even hurt me so bad during one time that I will never recover from the physical damage he did. I had to go to a doctor and have my wound looked at. I don't want to get too graphic but let me just say it was really bad.

So, he raped you? Yes! More than once! He was so strong and bigger than me so I could not fight him off. So I just laid there and let him do whatever he wanted to me.

Why didn't you leave him? I was scared of him and of what he might do to me and my family. Actually, I was terrified of him! The anger and abuse was so overwhelming that I could not function or even think straight. I started drinking so I would not have to think about what was happening to me. He choked me once too.

He tried and tried to get me pregnant I guess so he could own me and have total control over everything I did. He tried to control everything I did. He did not want me to work. He did not want me hanging out with my family. He didn't want me to graduate from high school. He did not want me to get a job. He even controlled how much I used my phone!

So I lied to my parents about everything. They did not know what was happening to me. He kept telling me that he just wanted me to stay home with him after we got married.

You thought about marrying him after all the abuse? Yeah I did.
I didn't know that it was supposed to be any different. I thought that
all that he did to me was okay, I didn't know. I just accepted what he
did but deep inside I hated all of it! I just didn't know what to do!

Why did you tolerate him abusing you? That's a good question and
I'm not sure I know the answer. I think, at first, when the physical and
sexual abuse started I though it would stop. I remember thinking too
that I wanted it to work out. When it didn't stop, but got worse, I was
paralyzed by fear that he would kill me in one of his rages.

I can't describe the overwhelming panic and fear I had when
I realized I was trapped. I was in a deep dark cave and I could not find
a way out. I was paralyzed.

Author's note: A complication to Ally's story.

The trauma was so severe and prolonged for Ally that she
developed an altar personality to deal with the overwhelming
abuse, fear, and confusion. This was uncovered after the first
few meetings I had with Ally.

The condition used to be referred to as Multiple
Personalities, but now it is called Dissociative Identity
Disorder. I worked under Dr. Collin Ross (Psychiatrists) with
those who had Dissociative Identity Disorder during my
internship of two years in the 1990's.

DID (as it is called now) means that a person, under sever
and prolonged trauma (most always sexual abuse and usually
at a very young age), develops one or more *alternate*
personalities to deal with the paralyzing emotions of fear and
confusion.

The presence of an *altar* causes disruptions of
consciousness and awareness and the person takes on a different
identity. The person is not aware of the presence of the
altar personality. The person with DID will have gaps in their

memory and do things that would not normally represent their behavior.

When an altar is in control of the person (host) they may become silent, withdraw, run, hide, or become aggressive. Once the altar ceases control of the host, the person will not remember events or their actions.

The main purpose of an *altar* is to protect the host from harm, specifically the abuse. There can be more than one altar personality present within the host.

Ally's altar personality was revealed when she told me that she heard a voice in her head. Ally explained that the voice talked to her about men and what she should do or not do. The voice was angry and aggressive. We decided to refer to her altar as *my friend*. No name has ever been given to her altar, just referred to as *my friend*.

The *friend comes out* or *speaks up* when Ally feels threatened or she hears a man's loud voice.

Tell me an incident when your friend came out. Sure. One time I was at a small social gathering when a guy suddenly shouted out. I don't remember what he said but it was quick and very loud!

I didn't know what had happened at that moment but was told later. I was told that I immediately bolted out the door and ran for two blocks extremely fast before I was caught by a guy friend of mine. By the time my guy friend caught up with me "my friend" withdrew. I'm thinking she knew I was now out of danger. I felt safe with the guy that ran after me.

How did you get away from him?

He was sent away for eight months (military) and during that time I decided that I needed to end the relationship. I realized that I had been happier and smiled more while he was away. I gained a little weight which I needed because I was not eating while I was with him. I got comfortable with the idea of leaving him and that helped me a lot. When he came back I met with him and as he was taking me home I told him in the car.

How did he take it? Well, better than I thought. I was afraid of him and worried what he might do to me and my family. He just drove off and that was it! I only saw him once after that some many months later.

How long did you wait before the next relationship?

Well, I waited about a year. Jimmy was a totally different person than Dillon. It was like a normal relationship and I did not know how to act at first. But that didn't last long.

How long did the relationship last?

Three and a half years. *You mentioned the relationship felt normal but didn't last. What happened?* Well we started arguing about six months after we started dating. And this went on for two and a half years!

What did you argue about? Stupid stuff, always stupid stuff. I thought he was pulling away from me and I didn't want that to happen.

What did you do to keep the relationship?

He broke up with me several times but I kept seeing him for, well you know. One time I even moved in with him and his parents. That was great. It was my first experience of being independent from my parents. I even asked him to marry me but he said no.

During the times he broke up with me I would still call him and hang out with him. He was still pulling away from me even though he was still getting what he wanted from me. I was good with that and I really though I could get him back that way.

Did it work? It did for a while but eventually it wasn't enough to keep him with me. I was very emotional a lot. During my time with him and the breakups I tried to hurt myself ten times.

Were you serious? Yea I was. But crazy things would happen to interfere with what I tried. *Are you glad it turned out like it did?* Oh for sure! It was just an emotional reaction.

How did the relationship end?

Well that was the worse day of my life! It all started around 6:00 P.M. with an argument with my parents that got really nasty. I had been drinking ... a lot! I locked myself in the bathroom and sat in the bathtub. I was very upset. Dad was beating on the door for me to open it so they could come in. I refused. Dad broke the door in and they rushed to see if I was okay. Mom got in my face and I slapped her. It got so bad that I called the police. They didn't abuse me I was just angry and out of control.

What did the police do? Nothing really. One officer gave me his card if I needed anything. That was nice.

Well, after they left we got into another argument. This time I left running out the door. All I had on was my pajamas, no shoes. I had my phone too. I ran fast and didn't stop for two and a half miles! I finally stopped in a school parking lot. I was tired!

My parents called Jimmy to find me. Jimmy called and I answered and told him where I was. When he got there I started telling what had happened. I couldn't believe it but after all that had happened with my parents Jimmy broke up with me in the car!

I went crazy! I got on top of him and begged him to not break up with me. I told him I would change. Give me another chance I kept saying! He would not! He took me home.

Dad met me at the door and picked me up and told me that whatever I needed he would do! When I needed him the most he was there for me!

What do you want the readers
to learn from your story?

After a bad relationship, focus on yourself to become sufficient within yourself. You can make yourself happy. You do not need to rush into another relationship. Take some time.

Author. Ally, thank you for sharing your story. You like, Nichole and Maddy, have endured unthinkable difficulties in life and have survived.

As I have said to you many times that you always land on your feet! Your unique story, like Nichole's and Maddy's, will help countless girls to navigate successfully through overwhelming thoughts and emotions as you have.

PART THREE

WHY DO GIRLS CHASE GUYS AFTER A BREAKUP?

Author's Note

I became aware of the extreme reactions of some girls after a breakup when I worked as a therapist in a mental health hospital in Dallas, Texas in the 1990s. I worked with all age groups and disorders at the facility but specifically with those in intensive care.

My duties included going to area hospitals in Dallas county to evaluate those in the ER due to psychological trauma. I had to decided whether or not the individual needed to be committed to the mental health hospital for their safety. I made 957 visits. The majority of the visits concerned young women (and some guys) who had attempted self-harm because of the breakup of a relationship. Their ages were from the teens to the thirties. I evaluated each one and found that the relationship, over which they had an extreme emotional reaction, was on the average, just three months old; the range was from two weeks to five months.

Since the 1990's I have worked with more young ladies that also had a severe and prolong reaction to the breakup of a relationship.

I was puzzled as to why attractive, intelligent, and creative young ladies would submit themselves to a toxic relationship. I was more concerned when I discovered the extreme things these girls would do to regain the relationship once it dissolved. I was driven to understand why.

I probed for answers and discovered that these girls shared what proved to be common themes in their temperament, home environment, and choices.

Although these three areas will explain their behavior, not all the girls shared everything that will be discussed to the same degree. It is, however, in the following three areas that we gain understanding of why a girl would do extreme things to retain or regain a toxic relationship that ended not of their choosing.

Chapter 8

TEMPERAMENT

The first area that these girls shared in common was they had the same temperament.

What is Temperament?

The word *temperament* refers to your natural and normal way of responding to people and events. Each person is born with one of the four primary temperaments commonly referred to as Choleric, Sanguine, Phlegmatic, and Melancholy.

The idea of temperament was popularized by Hippocrates (the Father of Medicine) 2,400 years ago. He said people are divided into four categories as shown below.

Each of the four primary temperaments takes a different behavioral approach to life. Each of the four temperaments have different levels of emotion that are expressed differently.

Choleric | The Choleric is *extroverted*, quick thinking, active, practical, strong-willed, easily annoyed but quickly calmed. They are naturally result-oriented. They are confident, brief, direct, and to the point when communicating with others. The Choleric has a huge ego, a firm expression, and they are self-sufficient. They are decisive, opinionated and find it easy to make decisions for themselves as well as for others. The Choleric is sociable for a reason (usually to get others to help them get results).

Emotional expression is triggered when the Choleric does not get quick results.

Examples of a Choleric include President Donald Trump and the former governor of New Jersey, Chris Christy.

The Choleric temperament is not frequently found in society so they are the fewest in number. Female Cholerics are extremely rare.

Sanguine | The Sanguine is *extroverted*, friendly, impulsive, fun-loving, activity-prone, entertaining, persuasive, easily amused, optimistic, and people-oriented. The Sanguine tends to be competitive and disorganized. The voice of the Sanguine will show excitement and friendliness. They have a natural smile and will usually talk easily and often. They are animated, excitable, and accepting of others. They build relationships quickly and have lots of friends. They find reasons to be around other people.

An example of a Sanguine is actor Will Ferrell; played Elf in the Christmas movie *Elf*. Emotional expression is triggered when the Sanguine has been rejected or embarrassed. The Sanguine temperament is very visible in society because they are people-oriented.

Phlegmatic | The Phlegmatic is *introverted*, calm, unemotional, slow moving, easygoing, accommodating, and service-oriented. The Phlegmatic is passive, routine, loyal, and non-emotional. They have a stoic expression (flat affect) and rarely smile. They are slow to warm up and indirect when interacting with others. The Phlegmatic lives a quiet, peaceful, routine life, free of the normal anxieties of the other temperaments. They avoid getting too involved with people and life. They prefer a few close friends and one-on-one relationships.

An example of the Phlegmatic is actor Bob Newhart; played Papa Elf in the Christmas movie *Elf*. Any demonstration of emotion on any level is rare for the Phlegmatic. They avoid conflict by being accommodating.

Melancholy | The Melancholy is *introverted*, logical, analytical, factual, detailed, private, conscientious, timid, organized, and quality-oriented. The Melancholy will (most always) have a serious, even concerned, expression. They usually respond to others in a slow, cautious, and indirect manner. They are self-sacrificing, creative, and can be a perfectionists. The Melancholy has high standards to avoid mistakes. They need a reason to be with others socially. Actually, they usually find reasons *not* to be with others. The are private people and prefer only a few close friends. They are not trying to *be right*, they are driven to *know* what *is* right. The Melancholy is a deeply feeling and passionate person. An example of the Melancholy temperament is Ben Carson; United States HUD Secretary.

Everyone has a combination of all four temperaments and the alignment never changes. Each person has a *primary* temperament followed by a *secondary* temperament and then a third and fourth. A person's behavior is best understood when your primary and secondary temperaments are identified. Notice the chart below.

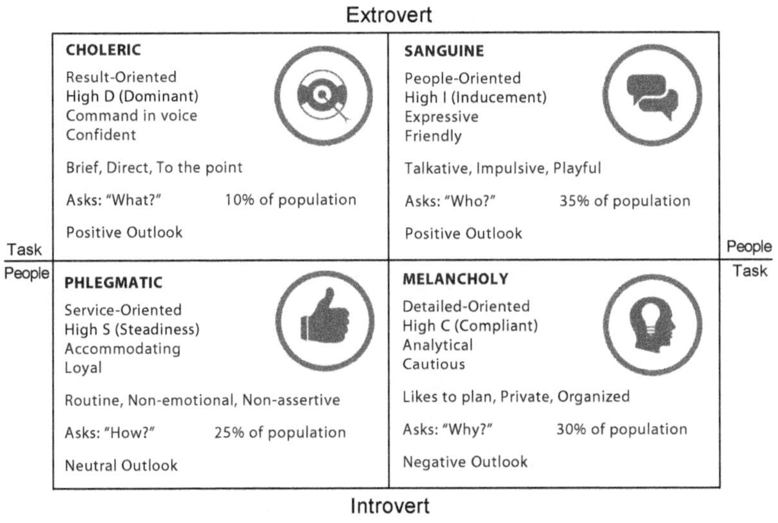
Extrovert
CHOLERIC
Result-Oriented
High D (Dominant)
Command in voice
Confident
Brief, Direct, To the point
Asks: "What?"
10% of population
Positive Outlook
SANGUINE
People-Oriented
High I (Inducement)
Expressive
Friendly
Talkative, Impulsive, Playful
Asks: "Who?"
35% of population
Positive Outlook
Task
People
People
Task
PHLEGMATIC
Service-Oriented
High S (Steadiness)
Accommodating
Loyal
Routine, Non-emotional, Non-assertive
Asks: "How?"
25% of population
Neutral Outlook
MELANCHOLY
Detailed-Oriented
High C (Compliant)
Analytical
Cautious
Likes to plan, Private, Organized
Asks: "Why?"
30% of population
Negative Outlook
Introvert

Why Is Temperament Important?

It is important to know your temperament because it will explain, in part, the strong emotional response to the breakup of a relationship.

My work at a mental health hospital and as a therapist in private practice revealed that those with the strongest emotional reaction to the perception of being *rejected* are Sanguine-Melancholy. Every one of the girls I've worked with over the years that had a strong and prolonged reaction to a breakup was Sanguine-Melancholy, no exceptions.

Why is this so? When the Sanguine (the excitable temperament) is combined with the Melancholy (the deeply feeling and analytical temperament) it produces a person who is *naturally* highly emotional and they have a natural fear of being rejected.

The Sanguine-Melancholy has the entire range of human emotion; they can get more excited than anyone and they can get down lower than anyone. It is, therefore, easy to see that their reaction to the *perception* of being rejected is more severe and painful.

Of course girls with another temperament can have emotional pain over a breakup but it's usually not as severe as the Sanguine-Melancholy nor does it last as long. Girls with another temperament combination will deal with the breakup quicker and will usually not seek counseling. It will happen on occasion but not as frequently as with the Sanguine-Melancholy.

The Sanguine-Melancholy Temperament

The Sanguine-Melancholy is driven by two natural needs. The primary need is to be *accepted* socially. The secondary need is to do things *right*. Either need may dominate their behavior depending on the requirements of the situation.

When the Sanguine and the Melancholy natural tendencies are combined, it produces a people-person who is sensitive, creative, and detail-oriented. The Sanguine-Melancholy is more emotional than the other temperament combinations. This combination is naturally able to *perform* in front of others to meet the need of the moment. And they also tend to have a higher IQ. Actually, those with a "genius" level IQ are almost always Sanguine-Melancholy with rare exception.

Description

The Sanguine-Melancholy needs to be with people *most* of the time but *some* of the time they need to be alone. When alone they will likely think, review, plan, or be creative. They need information, time to think and a plan before they can function effectively. They function best when they have a detailed plan. Once they have a plan, however, they may not be consistent or follow through because of a fear of failure.

The Sanguine-Melancholy has a very active, vivid imagination causing them to be creative in many areas like music, the performing arts, writing, decorating, problem solving, etc. They tend to be very image conscious and actively seek recognition for their achievements.

They have a deep need to know that they will be accepted by others. They may struggle with guilt feelings. They are usually well organized. Being organized does not necessarily mean that everything is neatly in place. Being organized can also mean that you know where everything is located — if you know what's in the piles then you're organized!

They have difficulty going to sleep because they are processing their thoughts; reviewing, planning, fretting, or creating. The Sanguine-Melancholy's emotions will likely fluctuate widely, especially if they are embarrassed or they have been rejected. They can do many things to an extreme.

The Sanguine-Melancholy tends to warm up slowly to new people because they are unsure of how they are being received. Once they feel safe or accepted they become more friendly.

Strengths

The Sanguine-Melancholy has a natural ability to function well socially (once the fear of rejection has been removed) and privately. They need to be with people but they also need to spend time alone. Their alone time allows their creativity to be expressed and developed ... but they do need time away from people. They process information quickly.

Many have the ability to excel in any artistic field. They have a high drive to win. They persuade others with facts and emotion. They are driven to do a task correctly and make a good impression in the process. They are capable of being the best in their chosen field.

Weaknesses

The effectiveness of the Sanguine-Melancholy in relationships and productivity in their career is often hindered because of giving into a variety of fears, such as the fear of being rejected, the fear of losing, and the fear of being embarrassed or disrespected.

They often react with extreme emotion if a fear is realized or they perceive something may happen that will be embarrassing. They may demonstrate intense emotion, become critical and condescending, get verbally (sometimes physically) aggressive, and will want to remove themselves from the situation. They also tend to have emotional highs and lows fueled by critical thinking, being impractical, having high standards, and failure to spend sufficient time alone.

Needs

The Sanguine-Melancholy will be at their best and will be highly motivated if their natural, basic needs are met, such as being with people, feeling accepted, and spending time alone to think, review, plan, and be creative. The amount of daily alone time needed varies with the individual — all will need some time alone but some will need more than others. They need a variety of activities and public recognition for their accomplishments.

Fears

Fear tends to create anger. Fear is a primary emotion and anger is a secondary emotion. The Sanguine-Melancholy may respond with extreme emotion if any of their natural fears are realized; such as being rejected, being embarrassed, losing, not doing the task correctly, not making a favorable impression, or being criticized personally (especially in front of others).

Creative

The Sanguine-Melancholy is the most creative of all the temperament combinations. With their deep emotion and vivid imagination they may draw, paint, write, compose songs, write poetry, sing, dance, decorate, do woodworking, photography, etc.

Those who are not involved in expressing their creativity this way tell me they do creative problem solving. Their creativity may also appear in the clothing they wear. They tend to dress fashionably and can even be flamboyant. In some way they will express their creative and colorful mind.

They are at their best when they are involved in a creative project that represents their interest. When motivated they will do as good as, if not better than, anyone else in their chosen field.

Emotional

If all emotions could be measured on a scale from one to ten, the Sanguine-Melancholy would have the entire range from top to bottom. They can express the top of the emotional scale and get extremely excited and the bottom of the scale and get severely depressed. This natural ability is what enables them to perform as actors and actresses.

Because they feel so deeply, it is no surprise that they usually bring intense passion to whatever they do with their life. They feel with more intensity and depth than all the other temperament combinations.

This deep well of emotion within may spontaneously erupt without warning. They can usually cry easily and often over the slightest disturbance. Surprising those around them, they may also become quickly agitated over the slightest thing and have a strong emotional reaction.

Guitar

It is not unusual for them to play (or want to play) the guitar. They will almost always teach themselves how to play this instrument.

Sleep

The mind of the Sanguine-Melancholy is very active and never seems to stop processing information. Because of this they often have difficulty going to sleep and staying asleep. One told me, "Thoughts are flying around in my head like the ball in a pinball machine and my mind lights up the score board with thoughts."

They are thinking about the day, planning tomorrow, pondering why this or that happened, investigating what might happen, and even try to figure out what to do if this or that were to happen. They tend to analyze everything that happens to them or about them, then they will analyze what they have just analyzed!

Summary

The Sanguine-Melancholy is *naturally* intelligent, creative and emotional. Girls with this temperament are the ones most likely to have an intense and prolong emotional reaction after the breakup of a relationship that was not of their choosing.

Will every Sanguine-Melancholy girl have this kind of reaction? Of course not. Some will make different choices, not express extreme behavior, recover in a reasonable amount of time, and move on with their life.

Young ladies with another temperament can have emotional pain over a breakup but it's usually not as severe nor does it last as long. Girls with another temperament combination usually deal with the breakup quicker and will usually not seek counseling. It will happen on occasion but not as frequently as with the Sanguine-Melancholy.

The Sanguine-Melancholy girl is susceptible to her early home environment especially between birth to age five.

Author's note: I have written a number of books and manuals on the subject of temperament. Two books that will help you understand the temperament concept are: *1) Why We Do What We Do, New Insights Into The Temperament Model of Behavior.* This book discusses the history, ten principles, common questions, and information on the twelve temperament combinations. *2) Born With a Creative Temperament.* This book is about the Sanguine-Melancholy.

"The greatest challenge in life is discovering
who you are. The second greatest is being
happy with what you find."
Muzictomyears.com

Chapter 9

HOME ENVIRONMENT

The second area that these girls shared in common was they had a similar home environment.

Unhealthy Home Environment

These Sanguine-Melancholy girls were exposed, to some degree, to the behaviors discussed below.

Anxiety

When one or both parents show anxiety when life throws a curve, it teaches children that you don't *solve* problems you just *worry* about them. Anxious behavior does not model nor teach how to develop problem solving skills. To make matters worse, some parents turn to medication (prescriptions, alcohol, etc.) to calm them because they are so worried that the outcome of their concern will not be favorable. Often, depression follows prolong anxiety. There is an ancient proverb that states, "Anxiety in the heart of man causes depression."

Anger

When parents show angry toward each other the children will naturally think it's okay to get angry with others when things do not go their way.

Being exposed to the angry outburst of parents, the Sanguine-Melancholy girl will fail to develop appropriate, effective, and calm ways of settling a disagreement with their parents and other children.

Angry parents will also yell at their children which gives the children permission to yell at others when they can't get their way. Children of angry parents are less empathetic and fail to develop overall adjustment skills. There is a strong relationship between parental anger and delinquency among teens.

The effects of parental anger can continue to impact the child into adulthood. This may show up in having difficulty in relationships, bouts of depression, social alienation, spousal abuse, career and economic achievement.

Arguing

It does not matter what the arguments are about, it's the fact that arguing takes place in the family that is the problem.

When parents argue in front of their children it creates fear and confusion within them. Arguing is selfish and teaches that making your point is more important than having a peaceful discussion and resolution. Arguing gives the children permission to argue to settle a disagreement with their parents, siblings, and friends (and eventually their employer).

Alcohol and Drug Use

When parents use alcohol or drugs (prescription or street) to escape coping with people or life events it teaches children to avoid facing the issues of life.

Abuse

When the above behaviors are present in a family what follows is often verbal, physical, and sometimes even sexual abuse.

Allowed Too Much Freedom

No guidelines, restraints, boundaries, and *do what you want to do* teaches I'm not significant enough for you to teach me how to live my life.

Inconsistent Discipline

Over the many years I have worked with these young ladies many have reported the discipline they received was given in anger or was extreme. Some reported the discipline they received was either inconsistent, too much, or not enough. Many have said they deserved the discipline but it did not match the issue.

Alienation

When the above behaviors are present in a family the Sanguine-Melancholy girl will feel alienated from the family but especially her father (or father figure). This is a major issue and core to the Sanguine-Melancholy's drive to chase a boy after a breakup.

Criticized

When the Sanguine-Melancholy is routinely criticized it teaches the girl that "I'm not enough," "Something is missing or I would not be criticized!" Criticism is received by the Sanguine-Melancholy as *rejection.*

I recall an incident that occurred with my daughter when she was around age five. I was helping her color a page in her coloring book and noticed that she was going outside of the lines. My intention was to help her see that she needed to stay within the lines of the image she was coloring. So I pointed out softly "Let's stay within the lines." She was very offended and snapped back, "You can't color good!" I was momentarily stunned at how my message was received but quickly corrected my mistake and said "You color it anyway you wish sweetheart." She approved of my new message, recovered, and continued her masterpiece!

Now my daughter is not Sanguine-Melancholy, she is a Sanguine-Phlegmatic. But that taught me how sensitive a child can be to perceived criticism. It is so important to be encouraging.

Compared

When a Sanguine-Melancholy child is compared to someone else, i.e., "Why can't you be like ...?" or "_____ doesn't act like that!" or "Why can't you just sit there like _____ and not _____ so much?"

When these kind of messages are delivered from parents it is received by the Sanguine-Melancholy girl as *rejection*. The child feels like...

"There must be something wrong with me or
   I would be like_____!"
"Someone else is being viewed as better than me!"
"Someone has to win and somebody has to lose in order
   to be valued."
"I have to perform to my parents standards to be loved."

When siblings are present these kinds of messages create rivalry, pitting child against child to see which one gets more praise or attention from mom and dad. The Sanguine-Melancholy often develops resentment toward the one with whom they are compared.

Condemned

The Sanguine-Melancholy, often, from a very early age is different than other children. They tend to walk early and talk early. They can seek being the center of attention in various ways from misbehaving, wearing makeup early, dressing up, talking loudly, singing, displaying excessive energy, getting very excited, wanting to be involved in sports or just anything to get attention! These behaviors are an attempt to prove their value to her parents. The message is "Don't condemn me, accept me for who I am!" When the Sanguine-Melancholy girl is criticized, compared, or condemned because of their "difference" the results can be devastating to the child. I have been told things like:

"I could not be different growing up!"
"I had to be like my parents or I was not accepted!"
"I can't have my own ideas!"
"I can't be me!"

"I'm not enough!	"I'm not pretty!"
"I'm unlovable!	"I am stupid!"
"I am defective!	"I always fail!"
"I'm no good!	"Something is wrong with me!"

The impact on such an environment is potentially very damaging for any child's healthy development. When the Sanguine-Melancholy is exposed to these conditions the potential impact is severe and long lasting. They have the emotional ability and drive to strike out and strike back and to find someone that will accept them for who they are.

Healthy Home Environment

In his insightful book, *The Sensation of Being Somebody* (1975, Zondervan Publishing House), Dr. Maurice Wagner (1914-2005) identified three necessary feelings we must experience to form a healthy self-concept. These are universal and timeless needs that everyone has. They are the feelings of ...

Belongingness (I'm in)
>   Worthiness (I count)
>   Competence (I can)

Three Necessary Feelings

The following are excerpts from Dr. Wagner's book, pages 32-37. These three feelings integrate to form the essential elements of self-concept. They not only constitute the mental structure of self-concept but give it support and stability.

> These three feelings blend together in the formation of self-concept like three tones of a musical chord. At times each can be considered separately, but usually it is impossible to distinguish one from the other. As in a musical chord, the first note, or root, is fundamental; so with self-concept, the sense of belongingness is primary and fundamental to the development of the other two elements.
>
> The three feelings also work together like legs of a tripod to support and stabilize self-concept. If any one of the three feelings is weak, the self-concept totters like a camera on a tripod when one leg is slipping.
>
> Each of these feelings is developed on a fundamental level in early childhood during the impressionable years. As one approaches adulthood and the state of responsible independence, he functions from this fundamental base of self-concept feelings.

Belongingness (I'm in)

Belongingness is an awareness of being wanted and accepted, of being cared for and enjoyed. It is the "part of," or "we," feeling experienced when we sense we are wanted or desired by some person or group of people.

It is natural to want to be "in" with the people we admire. We tend to maneuver and manipulate to feel accepted by them. We watch for evidence of their personal interest in us. We may work to capture their attention. In the final analysis, however, they must take the initiative to make us feel accepted, or we doubt if they really wanted us.

Our sense of belongingness is fundamentally established in infancy. Children develop feelings of belongingness when loving parents anticipate their discomforts and affectionately provide for their needs. A tiny infant is sensitive to being loved. When she is loved in her first year, she develops an essential trust in the goodness of life and the dependability of people. This prepares her for better adjustment in future childhood years and for a happier life.

Worthiness (I count)

Worthiness is a feeling of "I am good, or, I count, or, I am right." We feel worthy when we do as we should. We verify that sense of worthiness when we sense others' positive attitudes toward us and their hearty endorsement of our actions. When others do not approve but criticize us, we feel a loss of worthiness and self-esteem. This usually makes us defensive or angry. We will probably attempt to justify ourselves to recover our lost sense of worthiness and self-esteem.

Worthiness is related to a sense of not only being right but doing right. Self-control is important to worthiness. Worthiness relates to belongingness, for we feel good about ourselves when we are accepted by others. Worthiness is a function of our sense of self-esteem.

We like to believe we are capable of good decisions. In defense of our sense of personal worth, we quickly blurt out,

"You don't understand." Then we proceed to set the accuser or the adviser straight. If we have no immediate explanation, we might in exasperation try to recover our worth with "Why don't you mind your own business!"

Some people would rather comply with their critics than risk a confrontation. In being agreeable they presume to have a sense of worth by maintaining the good will of the other person. Some do it by attacking others, telling them where they are wrong. Some give advice; whether or not they have been asked for it. In their sense of mastery over others, they verify for themselves a peculiar sense of worthiness.

Some comply to preserve their sense of worthiness. They are afraid of losing more by confronting and defending than by giving in. Still others are so intimidated by the positive attitude and critical approach of certain people that they try to preserve their sense of worthiness by making practically no decisions at all. They continually ask for the opinions of others, even on simple matters. These people never developed a good sense of worthiness through making good decisions for themselves, and they are very dependent upon others.

Competence (I can)

This is a feeling of adequacy, of courage, or hopefulness, of strength enough to carry out the tasks of daily life-situations. It is the "I can" feeling of being able to face life and cope with its complexities. An immediate sense of competence derives from what is now happening, but there is also a general sense of competence that reflects the memories of accomplishments and failures of past experiences. Competence begins to develop in preadolescent years, but it grows on to a more fixed attitude as a person finishes her teens. Competence is affected positively by successes, negatively by failures.

Conclusion

Dr. Wagner concludes: "These three feelings work together to give a person a sense of identity, a self-orientation to living. Belongingness, worthiness, and competence are essential elements of self-concept and together they affirm to a person that she is somebody."

Three Natural Abilities To Develop

In chapter 5 of his book, *The Sensation of Being Somebody*, Dr. Wagner identifies three natural abilities that need to be developed early in the life of a child; empathy, identification, and love.

Empathy

Empathy is a fundamental talent that makes it possible, to relate to others emotionally. Every person is born with the ability to empathize. Empathy is the capacity to sense feelings by her body gestures and the intonations of her voice. Most of the empathic message comes through the sense of hearing. The ability to empathize by sight is less definite, and the ability to empathize through the sense of touch is less definite than the other two.

We all seem to understand the general mood of another person simply by hearing her voice and seeing her facial expressions. Emotional feelings are communicated from one person to another by empathy as well as by words. This intangible connection between two human beings is called empathic communication.

Empathy begins to manifest itself in the infant's behavior soon after she is born. It becomes the basis of nonverbal communication all through her life. Before the child is able to understand the language of her household, she senses the emotions of the people near her. We see her responses and sense empathically that she understands. How much she understands is open to question. We know she enjoys being liked.

Identification

Identification results from being able to empathize and to remember. The word identification comes from the idea of two things the same. By empathy we sense another person's feelings; feelings remind us of similar feelings we once had. We instantly feel like we are like the other person, for we have feelings that are similar about the same kind of situation. Generalization also takes place; we do not think of being like the other person in just one specific aspect, rather we usually generalize our feelings and assume we are like him/her in many ways.

Identification brings the other persons attitudes into ourselves and they become part of us. We learn to do things or not to do things by identification. This is especially true of children who are in a dependent relationship with their parents.

Love

Love is an emotion that gives meaning and helpful purpose to relationships. It is a function of empathy and identification. We sense another person's feelings by empathy; as we identify with those feelings, we care about what is happening to that person as though it were happening to us. Love desires the same benefit for the other person as one would wish for himself. Love is an emotion whose dominant feeling is affection. The goal of love is the close association of another person with oneself.

Thus love shares in the other person's pleasures and is also sincerely glad for her happiness. Love also shares in her distresses and miseries and is sincerely sorry for her situation. Love motivates one to be helpful in promoting the other person's welfare. Sympathy and compassion are feelings of caring and are attributes of love.

Self-concept evolves during childhood as a result of loving relationships with parents and other members of the family. After a person grows to adulthood self-concept is verified and strengthened in loving relationships with peers. Loving relationships bring meaning and purpose and fulfillment into living regardless of one's age.

Conclusion

A healthy home environment in which one is raised is essential to developing one's self-concept. No home environment is likely to contain all of the elements to perfection as discussed by Dr. Wagner. It is, however, critical that these elements are mostly represented when raising a child.

The home in which these Sanguine-Melancholy girls grew up in mostly lacked these fundamental elements to some level. They were instead exposed to the behaviors discussed in first section of this chapter to some degree.

Chapter 10

RESPONSE TO YOUR HOME ENVIRONMENT

The third area that these girls shared in common was they had similar responses to their home environment.

In the previous chapter I contrasted some ingredients of an unhealthy home environment with a healthy environment. The intent was to show what the parents (or caregivers) do that can be either helpful or harmful to children during the impressionable years.

Much has been written about the parents (or caregivers) responsibility to provide a good environment for their children. There is, however, more to the story that needs to be told. We sometimes overlook a critical piece to the environment in which a child is raised. And that is the child's *perception* and *response* to their environmental influences.

Karen Horney, M.D. (1885-1952) believed that anxiety was the result of parental *indifference* towards the child. Dr. Horney placed importance on a child's *perception* of the relationship interactions with the child's parents.

Most only look at the parent's *intentions* when interacting with the child and exclude the *child's perception* of the communication. The *child's perception* of the communication is the bases of the child's *response* to her parents or caregivers.

The Sanguine-Melancholy's Response

I am not writing about just any girl's response to their home environment, I am writing specifically about the response of a Sanguine-Melancholy girl during the impressionable years.

The Sanguine-Melancholy girl is *highly* sensitive to how well she is being cared for, loved, spoken to, and accepted. She is, therefore, more vulnerable to the elements in her environment early in life. When a Sanguine-Melancholy girl is exposed to the negative behavior described in the previous chapter behavioral consequences will most likely occur.

Remember, the Sanguine-Melancholy's core fear is that of being rejected, put down, disrespected, or embarrassed.

> *For parents (caregivers).* If you are the parent (or caregiver) of a Sanguine-Melancholy consider this illustration: If I were to hand you two small bottles of a clear liquid. They look the same and both bottles are full of what appears to be water. You would take no particular caution handling either bottle.
>
> But if I told you one of the bottles contained water and the other one contained nitroglycerin you would handle that one much differently! If you understood the nature of nitroglycerin you would know that if was bumped or dropped it might explode. You could complain that the nitroglycerin ought not to be that sensitive! Or, you could accept the reality of the nature of nitroglycerin and treat it accordingly!

Like any child growing up, they want to be loved, accepted, and valued for who they are, as they are. When this doesn't happen, the Sanguine-Melancholy internalizes her feelings and develops beliefs that will help her make sense out of her experiences. These feelings and beliefs will guide and direct her the rest of her life if not altered.

Reminder. When a Sanguine-Melancholy girl is raised in an environment that includes the following kinds of behaviors and attitudes by the parents or caregivers it is highly likely that severe consequences will result.

Parents show anxiety about life events.
Parents show anger toward each other and/or the children.
Parents argue in front of the child.
Parents expose the child to alcohol and/or drug use.
Parents physically, verbally, or sexually abuse the child.
The child is criticized for not conforming.
The child is compared to other children.
The child is condemned for having different views.

The Sanguine-Melancholy girl, like a sponge, will likely soak up negative elements convincing her that something is wrong and that she was never enough to please her parents. The Sanguine-Melancholy has the emotional assertiveness and drive to strike out or strike back at those that she perceives are rejecting her.

I am not saying negative consequences will *always* occur, I am saying they are *likely* to occur on some level. The following responses are typical.

Feels Rejected

Use of the word "No!" The feeling of being rejected usually begins early in life. Most every parent will use the word "No" when directing, correcting, or redirecting their child's behavior. Some use that word with an edge in their voice or even express it in anger. Usually, nothing more is said after delivering the message "No!" The parent will usually not follow up with *why* the word "No" was used, just "No!" This may cause the child to become frustrated because they have not been told *why* the word "No" was used.

The little Sanguine-Melancholy girl *does not receive* the message of "No" as direction, correction, or redirection, she receives hearing the word "No!" as *rejection*! Hearing the word "No" and other sharp words the Sanguine-Melancholy girl will likely grow up feeling rejected by her family and especially by her father.

Of course, it's not the parents intent to reject the child by saying "No!" It's the way the child feels. Parents mean well when directing or correcting their child however the messages are delivered. What the young Sanguine-Melancholy girl needs but unable to ask for at a young age, is the reason "Why" she is being corrected, directed, or redirected. Of course, this is true of the male Sanguine-Melancholy as well. I explained this to a young adult male and he came up out of his seat and said with intense emotion "I was never told why!"

Communication is not what you say, it's what the other person hears. When the little Sanguine-Melancholy girl hears "No!" from her father (or mother) there will most likely be an immediate emotional reaction; sometimes anger, sometimes tears, and sometimes she will leave the room and hide (if she can walk).

Feels Alienated

When the Sanguine-Melancholy girl feels rejected it follows that they will not feel a part of the family. In the previous chapter I mentioned that Dr. Wagner wrote about the need for a child to feel like they *belong* in the family. If the child does not, they will then naturally feel estranged or alienated from the family.

Pressured to conform. Often parents will pressure the Sanguine-Melancholy to conform to their standards and views. Since they feel rejected and not a part of the family it fosters feelings of "I do not belong here!"

Because they feel rejected and alienated from the family they may develop different views than their parents on religion, politics, and the kind of friends they should have. They may dress differently, wear a nose ring, color their hair orange, stay up late (or all night), sneak out of the house, sneak boys into the house, smoke marijuana, and generally just rebel against anything the parents stand for. This is one way the Sanguine-Melancholy girl gets back at her parents for feeling rejected by them.

When the girl does not conform, sometimes the parents double down on rules making matters worse. Establishing more rules drives the Sanguine-Melancholy girl farther away from her family. Some even leave home to get away from the "oppression" they feel.

Feels Misunderstood

When the Sanguine-Melancholy feels rejected and alienated from her family she feels not *understood*. Worse, she feels *misunderstood*! She will fight to be recognized and accepted by her family or someone. She feels different and is confused as to why no one loves her for who she is!

Feels "It's Not Okay To Be Me"

Feeling rejected, alienated, and misunderstood, she decides that it's "Not okay to be *me."* The feelings deepen that "Something is wrong with me!" She gets more and more confused and frustrated. She then decides being different may help me get attention and be loved. As she gets older she acts out and starts doing more and more extreme things. She is trying to find out who she is because her family does not approve of her or her behavior. She thinks, "Who will accept me?"

Feels Disconnected From Her Father

When the conditions of an unhealthy home environment exist within a family one of the consequences that will often occur is a lack of connection with the girl's father or a father figure. The importance of a father connecting with his daughter cannot be overstated.

The following article is from the website *www.verywellfamily.com/tips-for-raising-a-girl-without-a-father-in-her-life-4126769*. Accessed 1-18-2020).

The plight of fatherless daughters has been gaining some attention on the part of social scientists and parenting experts in recent years. From a 2013 television episode on the Oprah Winfrey Network to ongoing social science research, the experts have been actively documenting the challenges that fatherless daughters face growing up, and how their experiences differ from girls who grow up with a dad in their lives.

Consider some of the impacts on a girl's life that come from the lack of a father as she is growing up.

Struggles with low self-esteem and feelings of unworthiness.
Lack of standards in her life as they relate to men.
Loss of a sense of security.
Lower levels of well-being.
High levels of anger-related depression.
Emotional challenges in intimate relationships.
Earlier sexual activity and teen pregnancy.
More likely to marry in their teenage years.
Much more likely to have a baby outside of marriage.
Much more likely to be divorced at some point in her life.

Whether a father is not in the picture due to death, divorce, abandonment, or incarceration, the challenges are still the same. And a mom or grandparent often ends up trying to fill the gap in a girl's life with varying levels of success.

Daughters learn from their fathers much of how they treat and respond to men. Dr. Linda Nielsen, author of the book *Embracing Your Father: Building the Relationship You Want with Your Dad* (2004), has identified several specific areas in which fathers typically have an equal or greater effect on their daughters' lives than mothers:

Creating a loving, trusting relationship with a man.

Expressing anger comfortably and appropriately,
  especially with men.

Dealing well with people in authority.

Being self-confident and self-reliant.

Feelings of worth or value.

For any girl, regardless of temperament, the importance of a deep connection with their mother and father cannot be overstated. According to Dr. Wagner, as previously discussed, *every* child needs to feel like they *belong* (I'm in) the family, and that they are *worthy* (I count), and that they are *competent* (I can).

As mentioned, these three feelings are the foundation upon which a child develops the ability to show empathy to others, identify with others, and show love to others.

I am suggesting that the Sanguine-Melancholy girl is the one more likely damaged the most because of the lack of connection with their father, especially their biological father. Remember, they have the deepest and most intense fear of being rejected. So they will react the strongest when they do not feel accepted.

Dr. Nielsen's claims correspond with the findings of Dr. Barry Ellis, a psychologist at the University of Canterbury in Christchurch, New Zealand. After interviews and observations involving several hundred girls over many years in both the US and New Zealand, Ellis found that the absence of a biological father correlated significantly with young girls' sexual behavior, including the incidence of teenage pregnancy.

While a father's absence doesn't directly cause a girl to act out sexually, it does appear to contribute to such behavior more significantly, according to the data from Ellis. A father's absence has a greater impact on a girl's development than temperament, personality, or even socio-cultural, and economic factors.

In a related study published in the Journal of Personality and Social Psychology, Ellis found that the age of puberty in girls corresponded significantly with the presence of the biological father: girls who interacted infrequently with their fathers entered puberty *earlier* than those whose fathers were consistently present.

While a few theories have been formulated to explain this phenomenon, the bottom line is that fathers do significantly affect their daughters' social and sexual identity — even at the biochemical level. (https://www.babble.com/parenting/dad-raising-little-girls/, accessed November 12, 2019.).

Feels Discouraged

The accumulative affect of a negative environment will often cause the Sanguine-Melancholy girl (or anyone) to be discouraged. This usually means they loose hope and their enthusiasm for living and will not apply themselves to develop their skills and creativity. They will often find other ways to escape the pain of feeling rejected.

Discouragement is often seen in a girl's attitude of "I don't care," or "I don't want to," or "You can't make me do that," or "I can't do that."

A discouraged girl may not do their school work (high school, trade school, college, etc.) to get good grades, or try hard at work to do a good job, or fail to keep their living area clean.

One young girl was so discouraged that she ask me "Is it worth it?" She was only thirteen and already questioned whether or not life was worth living! Her spirit was so wounded because she had been criticized and exposed to anger that was directed toward her. There was also alcohol abuse in the family.

Conclusion

When a Sanguine-Melancholy girl is raised in a negative environment and does not connect with her biological father, she is left with a void and longing in her heart. She will often feel rejected, alienated, misunderstood, and feel that "It's not okay to be "me." She becomes discouraged.

After puberty, she realizes that she now has a new tool to attract male attention, her sexuality. Her body has developed and her *brain* has now changed to become open to sexual things. It becomes biologically instinctive to use this new awareness to get the attention she longs for.

A guy comes alone, filling the void by giving her attention. He treats her like she is special, important, and valued to get what he wants ... and when he does he drops her to find another girl to conquer. She erupts into extreme behavior and the chase is on!

Chapter 11

FOR PARENTS

Okay, if you are the parents of a daughter that chased a guy (or is chasing) like described in this book you may be feeling a heavy responsibility for her behavior.

If you contributed to a negative environment for your children take responsibility for what you did. Forgive yourself and ask for forgiveness from your daughter. It's all that you can do.

Know this, regardless of the environment you created for your daughter she still made her choices. Your influence didn't *cause* her behavior. She made her own choices. Now you may be thinking if you had been a better influence she would not have acted the way she did. Could be true but you don't know that nor can you know that. She may have made the same choices or not. Here's an example.

Sue was raised in a Christian home with good, caring, and reasonable parents. She was a model teenager and never gave her parents cause for concern. Soon, that began to change. The closer she moved into her late teens rebellion began to show. By the time she reached twenty, she was drinking, smoking marijuana, and using other drugs. Later her mother found out that she was having sex with all the guys she dated. They were shocked, this was not the girl her parents had raised.

Some of the guys she dated were approved by her parents but not by Sue. She only used them for sex and attention as it turned out. Then she met Tim. The parents did not like him but that did not matter to Sue.

She moved in with him much to the disapproval of her parents. She acted like he had a spell over her. Nothing anyone could do made a difference with her. She was determined to be with him even though he treated her with a lack of respect and they argued all the time. He threw her out of his apartment a number of times but she always found a way back.

He threw her out one more time and this time she went home saying that she was finished. She finally believed what her parents and others were saying about him. He was dishonest, egotistical, narcissistic, and a fraud in how he presented himself. He routinely milked people out of money by deceiving them. She saw all of this but it did not matter until he threw here out this last time.

Deflated of her dream to live with him she returned home. She said that under no circumstance would she go back to him, "Even if he ask me." Then it happened. He called her and asked her to come back. She said "I didn't know he wanted me back!"

She turned her back on her family and married him. What would drive her to want to be with him after all he had done to her and her family?

So parents, even if you did all things right it could still turn out this way. Remember, every girl that gets involved in a bad relationship chooses to do so.

Several years after the marriage Sue came to her senses and was willing to admit her mistake. She divorced him.

PART FOUR

HOW TO MOVE ON
WITH YOUR LIFE

Chapter 12

TRAPPED AND DEPRESSED?

Once you get into a relationship it is difficult to let go, regardless of the reasons why you should. The difficulty increases when you are married and/or you have children together.

You may be asking "Why did I wait so long to do something?" The short answer is *what you needed from him was greater than the reality of his character.* A shorter answer is *you did not want to!*

Trapped

When you recongize that your relationship is toxic you may feel *trapped* not knowing what to do.

When feeling trapped, we either do not try to come up with a solution or we put off making a decision to solve the problem. You may also over think the situation and become stuck with the *paralysis of analysis.* Your thoughts just go around and around never deciding on a plan or solution.

Depressed

The second feeling is that of being depressed. You feel overwhelmed and you do not have clear direction. Depression of course can be very paralyzing, further trapping you into uncertainty, circular thinking, and inactivity. You are stuck! What do you do?

Feeling trapped and being depressed will hinder you from moving on with your life.

Are you struggling with whether or not you should end a toxic relationship, or how you should do it? These feelings can be overcome when you make a decision. Here are three choices to consider.

This is the last time I'm hurting myself
to make you happy!

Chapter 13

1ST CHOICE...

DO NOTHING!

That's right, stay with him. Choose to submit to him and let him continue to abuse you any way he wishes. Under no circumstances complain to anyone about anything he does to you or says about you. Do not defend yourself when he accuses you of something you did or said (knowing that you did not say or do what he claims). The reality is that these abusers look for someone else to blame so be that person.

Do not argue or disagree with him. Let him know he is right, not just this time but every time. Ignore the advice that people give you like "Get out of the relationship and move on with your life." Say only nice things to him and about him to others and never question his character or integrity. Also, accept the fact that he will lie all the time about most everything.

Accept that giving intimacy to you is conditional upon his needs, not yours. Quit asking others (even therapist) how you can make this relationship work. The rules are simple; his rules are the only rules. You must play by "his rules" not yours, your rules do not matter so stop complaining that he keeps changing the rules.

Accept that you may be the only one earning money. Support his spending habits and life style. Do not complain.

Keep secrets, don't tell anyone what is really going on. Do not complain if he changes your plans at the last moment; that's his right, not yours.

If this is your choice, be prepared to give up who you are and be willing to sacrifice what you care about the most. You will not be allowed to be yourself. Do not complain.

This sounds like staying means you cannot make a choice. That is incorrect. The choice you are making is to not have the right to choose.

> *Warning*: If you do everything his way, he still may
> end up moving on to another relationship.

Chapter 14

2ND CHOICE...

WAIT FOR HIM TO CHANGE

A relationship as discussed in this book will never be easy as you have already discovered. It can drain the life out of you. But for some reason moving on is not an option because your life is so wrapped up in the relationship. Perhaps because you have children together or that you really want it to work. Or, you do not want to lose the connection you feel with him. You are convinced he *may* change and you are willing to wait. You are hopeful that he will come to his senses. You beleive that he just needs more time!

If this is your choice then wait but with a plan. The plan should include getting him to a therapist, the use of medication depending on his behavior, and a date in which you will wait no longer. A firm date like three months from today if he is not improving then leave him. Give him your plan and the date. Do not tell him the plan or the date if you think he will have a strong emotional reaction and you would not feel safe.

Do not make the appointment with a therapist for him. If he is not willing to do it on his own then you have the answer that you're looking for. He doesn't care enough for you to get help with his issues.

Ask yourself, if he is the same as he is now in six months or a year from now would that be okay with you? Two years? How long are you willing to wait?

My Opinion

Is it possible for someone to make radical changes in *who* they are and *how* they behave? Of course! The better question is "How likely is it that a person will make radical changes in *who* they are and *how* they behave?"

As a therapist since the 1990's, I have observed that people do not change *much* and when they do change, it's *slowly*. I have also observed that when people change it's usually because of a *Significant Emotional Event* (SEE). This can be a positive or a negative event. Either has the power to move someone forward or backward.

Change can happen but the chances are "not favorable" for the guy described in this book. Is your guy the exception? Maybe, maybe not. Is it worth the risk to keep the relationship to find out? Maybe, maybe not. This is why you need to set a date for him to change significantly or you will move on. Decide exactly what he needs to stop or start doing. Write it down and keep it in a safe place. Do not set a date until you can firmly commit to it and will leave without his genuine compliance.

An ancient proverb states:
"Her value is more precious than jewels and her
worth is far above rubies or pearls."

Some girls do not understand what they are worth,
and some guys refuse to see what they have.

Chapter 15

3RD CHOICE...

MOVE ON WITH YOUR LIFE

You want to get beyond this toxic relationship? If so, then accept the responsibility for your choices and accept the reality of his character.

Accept Responsibility

Regardless of your natural temperament tendencies, regardless of your early home life, regardless of whether or not you connected to your biological father (or father figure), you still made choices to be in and stay in the toxic relationship.

You see, a parent can provide all the right ingredients for their child growing up and the child not respond favorably. Likewise parents may do all the wrong things in raising their child only for the child to not be severely impacted! We forget that the child makes choices too while growing up! Any child chooses their own response from an early age! There are no guarantees that any child will embrace (good or bad) what they are exposed to growing up.

One young lady many years ago told me that she had an extremely negative mother. If she said *day* her mom would say *night*. If she said *white* her mom would say *black*. Her mother was not only negative but oppositional.

One day the young lady said "I looked at her and said this is not my problem, this is her problem!" I responded with, "Wow, that's great!" I asked, "How old were you?" She said, "Five!" This young lady decided, at a very young age that she was not going to allow her mother to have a negative influence on her.

Another young lady came to me with an addiction and asked for help. I asked her why she was addicted? It surprised her a bit but quickly answered that she was in school and the pressure was just too much. I responded with "That's the wrong answer." I repeated the question, "Why are you addicted?" She reflected for a moment and said "It's my boyfriend, he drives me crazy!" I responded with "That's the wrong answer." She looked at me beginning to get a little frustrated and then said "It's my dad!" She then explained how mean he was to her! I responded again with "That's the wrong answer, "why are you addicted?" She was looking a little defeated and pondered the question more deeply. After a moment she seemed glad to finally have the answer. She said "It's my mom (who was sitting beside her) she's the reason!" I said "I'm sorry, that's the wrong answer." Raising her voice out of exasperation she said "Okay, you tell me, why am I addicted? I said, "Because you choose to be." She looked away, reflected on the answer and said "I never thought about that!" She left with her mother.

She came back two weeks later and said "I though a lot about what you said and I *decided* that if I chose to be addicted I could choose not to be!"

To get beyond where you are in your life make a choice to think differently as the girls did above.

Wisdom Quotes

Life is difficult especially when you're entangled in a toxic relationship. People have struggled throughout time with all kinds of different challenges. Some have left behind nuggets of wisdom to show us how to change our thoughts and control our emotions to get through life's difficult times. Here are some thoughts from Epictetus (c. 55 – 135 AD):

"People are disturbed, not by things or events, but by the views which they take of them."

"There is only one way to happiness and that is to cease worrying about things which are beyond the power of our will. "

"Man is not worried by real problems so much as by his imagined anxieties about real problems."

"The key is to keep company only with people who uplift you, whose presence calls forth your best."

"Any person capable of angering you becomes your master; he can anger you only when you permit yourself to be disturbed by him."

"Freedom is the only worthy goal in life. It is won by disregarding things that lie beyond our control."

"Circumstances don't make the man, they only reveal him to himself."

"He is a wise man who does not grieve for the things which he has not, but rejoices for those which he has."

Here are a few more wisdom nuggets:

> The degree of emotional pain you feel is related to
> the significance you put on the disappointment.

> A desperate heart will seduce the mind.

> When we are no longer able to change a situation,
> we are challenged to change ourselves.
>   Viktor E. Frankl (1905 – 1997)

> Life really does begin at forty. Up until then, you are
> just doing research.   Carl Jung (1875-1961)

> How can I look at this _____ so it's not a problem?

> Living life is not about everything turning out OK.
> It's about being OK no matter how things turn out.

> Life contains but two tragedies. One is not to get your
> heart's desire; the other is to get it. *Socrates*

> You will not be punished *for* your anger,
> you will be punished *by* your anger. *Buddha*

> You cannot reason with an unreasonable person
> so do not try!

> It would be nice if I had _____ but it is not necessary
> for my happiness!

> Accountability: It's not important WHAT happened,
> what's important is WHAT am I going to do about it!

> Staying trapped in your past will rob you of your
> future.

Accept Reality

A big step toward moving on with your life is to stop ignoring what you know to be true and accept the reality about him. Here's a glimpse of reality:

- ☐ Who he is going to be is not who he is. He is who he is.
- ☐ You saw him, not as he is, but how you wanted him to be.
- ☐ You loved him for the person he almost was, or for the person he was going to be.
- ☐ His character is flawed.
- ☐ He did not change because he did not want to.
- ☐ He is what he did, not what he said he will do.
- ☐ He separated you from your family and friends.
- ☐ He did not respect you.
- ☐ He did not value you.
- ☐ He did not love you.
- ☐ He controlled you.
- ☐ He lied to you.
- ☐ He used you.
- ☐ He verbally abused you.
- ☐ He used you for his pleasure.
- ☐ He does not deserve you.
- ☐ You deserve better treatment.
- ☐ He is a narcissist.

John Heywood (1546) said "There are none so blind as those who will not see. The most deluded people are those who choose to ignore what they already know."

Move On

To move on with you life you have to *accept* the *responsibility* for your choices and *accept* the *reality* of who he is (not who you thought he was). He took advantage of you and you allowed it to happen. People treat you the way you allow them to treat you.

You're not the only one that has had such an experience. There are three stories in this book that followed your same path. Learn from them. They shared their experiences to help you.

Memorize some of the wisdom quotes listed in this chapter. Pick the ones that are meaningful to you. Process your thoughts and feelings with someone you trust. Be determined to move on with your life.

Someone has said "The first step towards getting somewhere is to decide that you are not going to stay where you are!"

Zig Ziglar said "Getting knocked down in life is a given. Getting up and moving forward is a choice!"

I've learned that *the decisions you make turn around and make you.* Your life is the result of the choices you've made. If you don't like where you are, it's time to make better choices. Why not now?

Today is the first day of the rest of you life. Start it with a decision to move on with your life!

> "I always wonder why birds choose to stay in the same place when they can fly anywhere on earth. Then I ask myself the same question."
>
> quotesgram.com

Challenges are what make life interesting;

Overcoming them

is what makes life meaningful!

Chapter 16

HE IS A NARCISSIST

W hat's wrong with a guy who would do this to a girl? Why would a guy treat you as described in this book. Why would a guy use and abuse a girl, any girl? Why would a guy break off a relationship sometimes in a cold, insensitive, even cruel manner? Here are some thoughts to consider:

He may have been in the relationship to "get what he wanted" and once satisfied he just moved on.

He may have grown weary of the girl's emotional reactions which he caused by his own behavior.

He may have just grown tired of being in that relationship and decided to move on.

He could have found someone else he liked.

He could be a narcissist.

While working with these girls that have been abused, I was also able to work with some of the guys. They too possessed specific behaviors that were predictable. Not all had the tendencies to the same degree, but all these guys had similar behavior; they were selfish, self-centered, even self-absorbed.

Temperament

Every guy that abused a girl as described in this book was a Sanguine-Melancholy (who was self-centered). I cannot think of one exception. Of course not all Sanguine-Melancholy guys will behave this way; only those with a selfish heart; narcissistic.

Narcissistic Behavior

Another way to describe the behavior of a guy who would abuse a girl is to consider that he is narcissistic.

A narcissist is a prideful, arrogant, self-seeking person that is incapable of feeling empathy for others. They are takers not givers. They have an inflated sense of importance and seek attention from others in relationships and at work. They react to the slightest hint of criticism or lack of respect from others. Trouble follows them everywhere they go but they refuse to assume responsibility or accountability for their behavior; they blame-shift. Nothing is ever their fault!

It is impossible to be in a sustained relationship with them without consistently giving them not just attention but admiration. They mishandle money and often accumulate large debt. They are incapable of having a fulfilling relationship.

Narcissistic Behavior Professionally Defined

The classic symptoms of a narcissist personality are found on the website of the Mayo Clinic (www.mayoclinic.org) and are listed below:

Signs and symptoms of narcissistic personality disorder and the severity of symptoms vary. People with the disorder can:

1. Have an exaggerated sense of self-importance.

2. Have a sense of entitlement and require constant, excessive admiration.
3. Expect to be recognized as superior even without achievements that warrant it.
4. Exaggerate achievements and talents.
5. Be preoccupied with fantasies about success, power, brilliance, beauty, or the perfect mate.
6. Believe they are superior and can only associate with equally special people.
7. Monopolize conversations and belittle or look down on people they perceive as inferior.
8. Expect special favors and unquestioning compliance with their expectations.
9. Take advantage of others to get what they want.
10. Have an inability or unwillingness to recognize the needs and feelings of others.
11. Be envious of others and believe others envy them.
12. Behave in an arrogant or haughty manner, coming across as conceited, boastful, and pretentious.
13. Insist on having the best of everything — for instance, the best car or office.
14. At the same time, people with narcissistic personality disorder have trouble handling anything they perceive as criticism.
15. Become impatient or angry when they don't receive special treatment.
16. Have significant interpersonal problems and easily feel slighted.
17. React with rage or contempt and try to belittle the other person to make themselves appear superior.
18. Have difficulty regulating emotions and behavior.
19. Experience major problems dealing with stress and adapting to change.

20. Feel depressed and moody because
    they fall short of perfection.
21. Have secret feelings of insecurity, shame,
    vulnerability, and humiliation.

What Causes Narcissism?

No one knows for sure what causes the narcissistic personality disorder (NPD). The Mayo Clinic offers the following:

> People with narcissistic personality disorder may not want to think that anything could be wrong, so they may be unlikely to seek treatment. If they do seek treatment, it's more likely to be for symptoms of depression, drug or alcohol use, or another mental health problem. But perceived insults to self-esteem may make it difficult to accept and follow through with treatment.
>
> It's not known what causes narcissistic personality disorder. As with personality development and with other mental health disorders, the cause of narcissistic personality disorder is likely complex. Narcissistic personality disorder may be linked to:
>
> **Environment**? Mismatches in parent-child relationships with either excessive adoration or excessive criticism that is poorly attuned to the child's experience.
> **Genetics**? Inherited characteristics.
> **Neurobiology?** The connection between the brain, behavior, and thinking.

Risk factors. Narcissistic personality disorder affects more males than females and it often begins in the teens or early adulthood.

Keep in mind that, although some children may show traits of narcissism, this may simply be typical of their age and doesn't mean they'll go on to develop narcissistic personality disorder.

Complications. Complications of narcissistic personality disorder, and other conditions that can occur along with it, can include:

Relationship difficulties.	Physical health problems.
Problems at work or school.	Drug or alcohol misuse.
Depression and anxiety.	Suicidal thoughts or behavior.

Prevention. Because the cause of narcissistic personality disorder is unknown, there's no known way to prevent the condition.

Treatment

Treatment for narcissistic personality disorder centers around prolong therapy. Sometimes other diagnosis are combined with the disorder like bipolar, anxiety, depression, etc. In which case medication may prove helpful to keep the person calm while doing therapy. The NPD is difficult to treat because of their resistance to improvement; they do not see the need to change.

My Opinion

In my opinion, the cause of NPD is not the environment, genetics, or faulty brain chemistry. Since all behavior is a choice, it is the choices he made in his environment. The environment in which one is raised has influence on behavior but one still chooses the kind of person they want to be.

The core issue of one who has NPD is an intense fear of being rejected. They develop a false sense of importance to cover their fear of not being viewed as special. Their behavior is designed to protect their image by rejecting others before others reject them. They are consumed with themselves.

Can a Person Stop Being a Narcissist?

Anything is possible and anyone can change their behavior ... if they want to. In the case of one who is a narcissist, change is not likely to happen. The Mayo Clinic recognizes that treatment success is "unfavorable."

They are basically *change resistant* because it is a lifestyle way of thinking that begins early in life. They build a self-centered "world view" which is deeply embedded and entangled in their belief system. When the person is willing to consider change, improvement may occur.

Summary

The kind of guy that would abuse a girl as described in this work is, with rare exception, a Sanguine-Melancholy with a selfish, self-centered heart.

Again, not all guys with the Sanguine-Melancholy temperament will do this, but those who do are Sanguine-Melancholy with a level of narcissistic behavior. The chances of one who has NPD to improve are significantly unfavorable.

> "Withhold admiration from a narcissist and be dis-
> liked. Give it and be treated with indifference."
>
> Mason Cooley

Chapter 17

WHAT TO LOOK FOR IN A RELATIONSHIP

With a bad experience in your past you may be asking "How can I avoid getting into another toxic relationship?" Right question!

First, give yourself time to allow your emotions to settle down. How much time? The rule is that you know you're over something when you can talk about it without emotion. So if you still get angry or cry when you think about him and what he did to you then you're not ready for another relationship. If you get into another relationship too quickly it will be a rebound retaliation and those usually do not work. So, give yourself time and surround yourself with those who will give you support.

What Women Want From a Guy

First, learn from that toxic relationship and avoid any resemblance of anyone that reminds you of his behavior.

Next, do some research to expand your knowledge and awareness. Search the internet for articles about how to avoid a toxic relationship. Get a book that has been written on the subject.

Here is a list of things that girls/women have told me they want from a guy. Basically, they want to feel like they are number one in his life and not be controlled.

- ☐ Listen to me (most mentioned).
- ☐ Show me love.
- ☐ Show me attention.
- ☐ Show me affection.
- ☐ Accepted me for who I am.
- ☐ Hold my hand.
- ☐ Don't shun me around our friends in public.
- ☐ Understand me.
- ☐ Cherish me.
- ☐ Respect me.
- ☐ Give me freedom to express myself.
- ☐ Do not try to control me.

One young lady put it best when she told me"I want him to work on the relationship as hard as I do."

What To Look For In a Guy

Now, let's look at what to look for in your next relationship. Let's start with avoiding the type of guy that abused you! Pay attention to the warning signs! Also, avoid thinking "I want to help him *deal with his issues*." This is a trap.

Don't settle for less than a guy that is willing to work on the relationship with you and who treats you with respect. Qualities to look for include:

- ☐ Good relationship with his parents and others.
- ☐ Good reputation with friends.
- ☐ Work ethic.
- ☐ Gives and does not take.
- ☐ Has self-control (over emotions, money, etc).

- ☐ Accountable for his behavior.
- ☐ Respect for authority.
- ☐ Does not blame-shift.
- ☐ Does not rationalize.
- ☐ Reasonable.
- ☐ Sensible.
- ☐ Logical.
- ☐ Responsible.
- ☐ Patient.
- ☐ Kind.
- ☐ Makes me laugh.
- ☐ Respects me and my body.
- ☐ Able to give unconditional love.
- ☐ Grateful.
- ☐ Content.
- ☐ Makes good choices.
- ☐ Works and has a career path.
- ☐ Has a purpose in life.
- ☐ Similar age, socioeconomic background, education, political, and religious views.

I know finding a guy with *all* of these qualities is impossible. The point is to look for a guy that is *developing* these kind of qualities. He is out there so don't give up and do not settle!

> "I realized that I don't have to fight
> for a place in people's heart.
> If someone values me,
> they will keep a place
> in their heart for me."
> Dana Dawson

Chapter

18

SUMMARY & CONCLUSION

The reason girls chase guys after a breakup is they make a choice to do so. There are three factors that contribute to their decision to do extreme things in order to *retain* or *regain* a toxic relationship.

First, it's not just any girl that will do extreme things to retain or regain a bad relationship, it's most always a girl with the Sanguine-Melancholy temperament. Remember, the core fear of Sanguine-Melancholy is that of being rejected; i.e., embarrassed, slighted, put down, or disrespected. When it appears it has or will happen often strong emotion is released.

Of course, girls with another temperament will have difficult with the breakup of a relationship. The Sanguine-Melancholy, however, is the one more likely to have the greatest emotional display and for the longest amount of time.

The *second* factor is the Sanguine-Melancholy girl is born into a family where she preceives being rejected from an early age (usually before age five). She will carry into her teen years and beyond being very sensitive to the way people respond to her.

The *third* factor is a failure to connect to her biological father or a father figure. Connection needs to take place by age five. When it does not happen the Sanguine-Melancholy girl, equipped with the strongest desire of all the temperaments, will seek attention from males any way she can to satisfy their longing. They do not necessarily understand why they are so driven.

Apart from these three factors mentioned, a girl could stay in an abusive relationship because she loves him and believes it will work if she waits long enough for him to change.

The environment in which a child is raised may have positive or negative influence on their behavior. There is, however, no guarantee that positive influence will always have a positive impact on a child no more than negative influence will always have a negative impact. It will always be a choice the girl makes in how she responds to her environment.

I am saying that a girl's early home environment *may* have influence on their self-view, their world view of men, authority, etc.

I am saying that parents are accountable for the negative influences they exposed their children to when being raised.

I am saying that a girl raised in a negative environment is still accountable for the choices she makes. I am not offering an excuse to remove accountability for unwise choices by the girls that exhibit such behavior or the parents that contributed to a negative environment.

I am saying that regardless of the influences of their early home environment, these girls still made their own choices in deciding to be in a toxic relationship.

Do all girls make the choice to offer sex for attention? Of course not. Do all Sanguine-Melancholy girls have extreme reactions when a breakup occurs? Of course not. I am saying the girl most likely to have an extreme and prolong reaction to the breakup of a relationship is Sanguine-Melancholy.

Final Thoughts

If you are a parent, relative, or friend of a girl who is in, or who has been in, a toxic relationship, here's what you can do.

Understand her emotions run deep and it will take some time for her to process those feelings and her thoughts. Be there for her. Give her support and do not press her to deal quickly with all that she feels. It will take some time.

If you are a teenager, young adult, or beyond, and you have experienced a toxic relationship as discussed, just know that you are not alone. There are many others that have been entangled in a difficult relationship. You've read the stories of three girls that were able to learn from their experience and move on with their lives. You can too!

About The Author

John T. Cocoris has devoted his life since the 1970's to develop the temperament model of behavior. John has a B.A. from Tennessee Temple University, a Masters of Theology (Th. M.) from Dallas Theological Seminary, a Masters in Counseling (M.A.) from Amberton University, and a Doctorate in Psychology (Psy.D.) from California Coast University.

John established Profile Dynamics in the early 1980's to develop and promote the temperament model of behavior for use in business and counseling. He has been a management consultant since 1984 and has worked with a variety of companies giving seminars for training managers and sales people.

John has conducted seminars in churches to help church counselors help others. John has also trained other therapists in the use of the temperament model in counseling. John has been interviewed on the radio and has been featured numerous times on COPE, a national cable TV talk show. John and Phillip Moss formed Temperament Dynamics, LLC in 2017 to expand, develop, and promote the temperament model of behavior.

John has written many books and manuals about the temperament model including: Why We Do What We Do, New Insights Into The Temperament Model of Behavior; Born With A Creative Temperament, The Sanguine-Melancholy; 7 Steps To A Better You, How To Develop Your Natural Tendencies; A Parent's Manual To Helping Your Child Develop Their Natural Temperament Tendencies; A Leader's Guide To Using The Temperament Model of Behavior; How To Sell Using The Temperament Model of Behavior; The DISC II Temperament Assessment; The DISC3 Temperament Assessment; The Temperament Profile Assessment, and The Temperament Profile Assessment User's Guide.

www.ingramcontent.com/pod-product-compliance
Lightning Source LLC
Chambersburg PA
CBHW072138020426
42334CB00018B/1847